D0169982

"Perhaps because he has worked as a Christian leadership consultant in 11 countries, Kevin Treston has an amazing ability to pull together insights into leadership from a variety of sources: from Zen sayings to the gospels, from Plutarch to Stephen Covey. This book indicates that Treston is not merely a collector of wise sayings, however. He has integrated these insights and experiences into a wonderful approach to leadership in Christian communities that reflects the vision of collaborative ministry derived from Vatican II. This book would be especially useful as a resource for a parish staff to use over the course of several months as a basis for reflection and development."

Celebration magazine

"Readers will find here a quick refresher course and evaluation tool for their own pastoral ministry. It contains a discussion of leadership styles, models, skills, and characteristics, plus a chapter on co-leadership that articulates what a shared vision requires (a "fundamental agreement on core values," for one thing.) It also outlines some of the how-to's of collaboration (such as setting up organizational structures that clearly define roles and decision-making procedures). The final three chapters cover Christian leadership specifically, work as co-creation, and leadership for the next century."

Karen Sue Smith
Church magazine

"At a time when many Christian communities are seeking to discover a model for leadership that is both authentic to the values of the gospel and also effective in dealing with the attitudes and values of secular society, this compact but comprehensive introduction is a readable, valuable, and timely resource.

Theodore W. Bean, Jr.
Caregiver's Journal

"This new book from Australian writer and educator Kevin Treston grew out of his experiences of conducting sessions in schools, parishes, and hospitals. *Creative Christian Leadership*, seeks to link contemporary leadership theory with basic skills, all within the context of a Christ-vision for leadership."

Caravan, Canadian Catholic Conference
Religious Education Newsletter

"*Creative Christian Leadership* offers parish leaders, ministers, lectors, and councilors wise material on professional skills and the qualities of good leadership. The book examines the signs of the times and offers a hope-filled vision for a more cooperative style of Christian leadership energized by a vibrant spirituality."

Thomas More Book Club Newsletter

"Rooting his definition of leadership in Jesus' model of servant-hood, Treston explores the signs, images, formation, and spirituality of Christian leadership, focusing on the fundamental themes of other-centeredness and building relationships, urging us to live out the Christian calling conferred upon us at baptism.

This is one of the better volumes articulating basic Christian leadership concepts and skills. Its readability and brevity make it ideal for use by leadership teams in churches or organizations who wish to develop leadership from a Christian perspective."

Rev. Christine L. Nelson
Faith UCC, *Congregations*
Allentown, PA

CREATIVE CHRISTIAN LEADERSHIP

Skills for More Effective Ministry

KEVIN TRESTON

TWENTY-THIRD PUBLICATIONS
BAYARD ⊕ Mystic, CT 06355

Acknowledgments

Scripture quotations are from the *New Jerusalem Bible* published and copyrighted 1985 by Darton Longman and Todd Ltd., and Doubleday and Company Inc. and used by permission of the publishers.

Third printing 2000

Twenty-Third Publications
185 Willow Street
P.O. Box 180
Mystic, CT 06355
(860) 536-2611
(800) 321-0411

ISBN 0-89622-648-4
Library of Congress Catalog Card Number 94-62050
Printed in the U.S.A.

Contents

Introduction

This book is offered as a resource for all those who are involved in a leadership position that has a Christian perspective. We experience leadership in every facet of human life: family, school, business, parish, leisure, and social groups. All of us have been involved in groups that were animated by creative leadership. Unfortunately, we may also have endured leaders who were oppressive and ineffective.

Creative Christian Leadership: Skills for More Effective Ministry seeks to integrate the wisdom of contemporary theories of leadership with insights and practices of Christian spirituality. There is a significant convergence of ideas about leadership among such writers as Covey, Bennis, Sergiovanni, Senge, Kouzes, Ramey, Block, and the gospels of Mark, Matthew, Luke, and John.

As a consultant in pastoral ministry over many years in several countries, I have been both inspired and saddened by the quality of leadership in Christian agencies, especially in the areas of parish, school, health care, and social outreach.

Christian leaders inherit from Jesus a foundational principle for all leadership roles: "This is my commandment: love one another, as I have loved you" (John 15:12). However, this principle is all too frequently subverted by a dominant leadership style that is shaped by business and management models. In *Creative Christian Leadership* I propose theories and practices of leadership that are in accord with the teachings of Jesus and with the focused wisdom of contemporary writing about the nature of leadership.

There is an urgent need for creative leaders in our world. New paradigms of society and church are emerging which cry out for leadership that is at once imaginative and anchored in core values that respect the dignity of every person. We cannot leave today's and tomorrow's leadership formation to chance. We must be pro-active in ensuring that the leadership skills of our leaders are aligned to gospel values.

The scope of the book is designed to assist in the development of Christian leaders by providing commentary on nine key areas of Christian leadership. There are, in addition, suggested points for personal reflection on each of the nine areas.

The bibliography is in two parts. The first lists those books that are mentioned in the text; the second lists those titles that have in-fluenced me, which may also interest the reader.

Those in leadership positions may choose to study each chapter alone, and then explore the reflections with other members of the parish team, pastoral council, school faculty, hospital staff, or other organization. However this volume is used, may it help to en-gender study, reflection, and prayer on the leadership themes pre-sented here.

1

What Is Leadership?

Today, leadership is big news. Leadership courses abound. News bulletins on television and in newspapers analyze every facet of our political leaders. Books, videos, journal articles, and seminars on leadership attest to the perceived urgency by church and community groups to develop leaders who will respond creatively to a society and church in rapid transition.

Which leaders, living or dead, do you admire? Two people I esteem as leaders, separated by several centuries, are Jean Vanier and Hildegard of Bingen. Vanier's leadership draws people with disabilities into the circle of community. His L'Arche houses witness to the gospel value of inclusion. The extraordinary and courageous leadership of the medieval abbess Hildegard of Bingen inspires me. A feature of both Hildegard and Vanier is their fidelity to the way of compassion. What qualities do you admire in leaders?

Our contemporary world is crying out for moral leadership, since we are, in the view of many, at one of the pivotal points in history. The growing awareness of the health of our planet, the impact of global economics and technology, the explosion of population, the maldistribution of Earth's resources, the struggle for women's rights are just some of the signs of critical issues that confront our communities. We are living in times of new paradigm thinking about life-enhancing ways we might live as cooperative members of the Earth community. New social movements such as the search for economic or racial justice and peace and Earth-care ethics challenge a mechanistic view of world that restricts freedom and undermines the quality of life. Within our consumerist culture there is a deep yearning afoot for meaning that goes beyond the material and touches the heart. Authentic Christian leadership has much to offer a society bewildered by social fragmentation and a short-sighted lack of appreciation for all elements of creation.

For much of Christian history, leadership has been exercised by the episcopacy, clergy, and religious, with the laity as followers. In the last third of the twentieth century, a significant shift in church leadership has been taking place, slowly but inexorably. Collegial leadership, involving hierarchy, clergy, religious, and laity as fellow sojourners, is struggling to come to life.

The relative decline in the number of priests and religious, the impact of Vatican II ecclesiology in promoting the responsibilities of baptism, the increasing complexities of pastoral ministries, and a wide diversity of community needs are some of the influences motivating Christians to participate more actively in church and civic communities. The growing awareness of the role of women in society and church recognizes the limits imposed on the life of the Christian community by a patriarchal system of church leadership. Christians are being exhorted to exercise leadership in every facet of society. They are not to limit their Christian presence to the works and worship of the Christian community, but are to be a leaven in transforming the values of society regarding justice and harmonious relationships among ourselves and with our planet.

Definitions of Leadership

Everyone has some experience of leadership. In families, parishes, schools, social groups, and businesses, people take the initiative and get things done. Conflicts are resolved, obstacles eliminated, and people are motivated to achieve their goals. Contemporary discussions about leadership are concerned not with heroic leaders who live beyond the realm of mere mortals, but with ordinary men and women who daily carry out acts of leadership to help others attain their common goals.

Leadership is an elusive concept and means very different things to a variety of people. If you compare your list of preferred leaders with those of others, there would probably be big discrepancies between the lists. Popular misconceptions about leadership suggest that leaders are born, not made, that leadership is a rare skill, that leaders must be dominating people with a charismatic presence. How leadership functions concretely is difficult to describe because we often have different ideas of leadership and what makes a good leader. Each of us certainly knows when we encounter "good" or "bad" leadership, but it's hard to say exactly what leadership is. A leader you admire may be treated with contempt by someone else. Have you ever been surprised when someone has praised a leader whom you judged to be a very poor leader, no leader at all?

Leadership is not about "them" and "us"; "they" are leaders and "we" are not. In most situations, the real leader is actually the official, or designated, leader, such as the pastor, the school principal, the president of the pastoral council, the director of religious education in the parish. On other occasions, though, the actual leader of a group may be someone with a special talent for a particular and immediate task at hand. A breakdown in relationships within a community, a financial crisis, a drop in school morale may cast a previously unassuming person into the role of leader. I recall being very surprised on a school field trip when a reserved student suddenly assumed a capable leadership role to help me cope with an outbreak of sickness among the students.

History often records instances of the emergence of leaders in times of crisis. Winston Churchill rallied the British people during World War II with his stirring speeches of defiance against the Nazi terror. However, after the war, Clement Attlee, not Churchill, was elected prime minister of England, because the task of social reconstruction seemed to warrant a different kind of leader in England. Martin Luther King, Jr., Catherine of Siena, Archbishop Desmond Tutu, Hildegard of Bingen, Dorothy Day, and Mohandas Gandhi are people who spring to mind as outstanding leaders in very different social and religious environments.

There are countless definitions of leadership. Rather than settling on one particular definition, I propose a series of statements about the meaning of leadership that may illuminate its character. Each statement about leadership names some feature of it. Reflect on each statement and savor the aspect of leadership described.

Leadership is.
- influencing a group of people to achieve their goals.
- turning visions into actions.
- a creative relationship between task, leader, and members of the group.
- uncovering and illuminating ordinary things with new meaning.
- the art of motivating people.
- energizing others to do things.
- opening new doors of possibilities.
- nurturing dreams and transforming dreams into realities.
- empowering others and oneself to realize our potential.
- using the gifts of the group to fulfill its purpose.
- the art of managing resources.
- enabling people to move from intention to achievement.
- challenging the group to go from the present to a possible future.
- facilitating a reconstruction of world-views.
- making a difference.
- first walking the path you expect others to travel.
- exploring new questions rather than being comfortable with closed answers.
- being open to being personally transformed.
- inspiring others.
- uncovering the talents of the group and focusing these talents on the mission of the group.
- facilitating change.
- the transformation of followers to leaders.
- experiencing leadership from others.
- revealing the compassionate face of Christ.
- evoking hope.

A consideration of these statements about leadership confirms the view that although leadership is hard to define, there are certain fundamental themes that characterize what it is. For example, leadership is other-centered; it acknowledges and brings forth the gifts and dreams of other people. Leadership is not an exercise in ego inflation, but a creative endeavor to use the gifts of the Spirit in the community one is leading (1 Corinthians 12:4–11). Leadership is relational in that it honors the dignity of each person and does not permit the urgency of the task to subvert the value of each member of the group. Leadership does not consider the role of the leader as an exercise of personal power to fulfill one's political, social, psychological, or even religious aspirations.

Evolution in Thinking about Leadership

The story of how leadership has been understood and practiced throughout the ages is a description of how social, economic, and religious forces have shaped the style and nature of leadership. Every social group has some kind of leader. Over the centuries there have been shamanistic leaders who possessed mythical powers, elders in tribal societies, military commanders, emperors, philosophers, popes, monarchs, presidents, queens, and kings. In Plato's *Republic,* women were included in the social order but Aristotle considered them inferior beings and therefore unworthy to hold positions of leadership. During many centuries, the "divine right of kings" exalted leadership as an anointed mandate by God to rule. Louis XIV's famous dictum *L'état, c'est moi* (The state—it's myself) summed up the nature of absolute leadership.

The church community gradually lost its original tradition, that leaders—imitating Jesus—were to be at the service of those they led. Following the decree of Constantine in the fourth century, which recognized the legitimacy of the church throughout the Roman empire, church leadership assumed more the trappings of a monarchical, regal style of leadership, rather than its rightful servant style. The diversity of leadership in early Christian communities as expressed in many ministries began to be contracted into the single form of leadership as embodied in the clergy. According to the Whiteheads, in *The Promise of Partnership: Leadership and Ministry in an Adult Church:*

> As Christianity expanded during the third and fourth centuries, ministry began to shrink. The rich variety of charisms, scattered throughout the earliest Christian communities, was gradually absorbed into the ministry of priest. The powerful

gifts of teaching, healing, prophesying and community administration, were seen as belonging uniquely to the priest and bishop (p. 21).

By the Middle Ages, a clear dichotomy between clergy and laity had emerged with a two-tiered understanding of church leadership firmly established in church life: The role of the clergy was to lead; the role of the laity was to follow. One expression of this understanding of church leadership was clearly enunciated by Pope Pius X in 1906 in *Vehementer Nos*, para. 8:

> In the hierarchy alone resides the power and authority necessary to move and direct all the members of society to its end. As for the many, they have no other right than let themselves be guided and so follow their pastors in docility.

One feature of the Reformation churches was a more localized and shared experience of leadership. However, the greatest challenge to the belief in the divine right of leadership came from the era of the Enlightenment. Writers such as Descartes, Kant, and Voltaire proposed that reason, not authority, should be the governing force in society. To these philosopher-writers, authority was associated with blind obedience. For people to fulfil their destiny, Enlightenment writers said, reason—not dogma, experience, or tradition—would bring true emancipation. The French and American revolutions translated these ideas into political realities and the world was changed forever by such movements for democracy. Since that time, many of the debates about the nature of leadership in society and church have revolved around the way authority's power is exercised and legitimized.

How should authority in a school or parish be expressed? What kind of participation is most fruitful for decision making in the Christian community? How extensive is the process of consultation with the community before decisions are made?

The reaction against the demonic leadership of dictators such as Hitler and Stalin helped to stimulate the development of leadership theory after World War II. In the first phase of this development, research sought to identify the traits of successful/unsuccessful leaders. This "great leader" approach, or trait theory, postulated that certain character traits could be relied on as indicators of good leaders. During the 1960s more extensive research demonstrated that social environment, levels of maturity of the group, together with other significant variables, all shaped the nature and styles of leadership. From the two dimensional theories of Blake and Mounton (1964), where people and production were two key variables, Hersey and Blanchard (1976) added a third factor in leadership style: the psychological maturity of the group.

While a leader's attributes are always to be considered important factors in leadership styles, the focus of leadership theory began to move from the leader to the process of leadership itself. The emphasis on this process proposed that there is not one leader for all situations, but the possibility that in a given group one person might exercise good leadership in one set of circumstances and another person in another set. A critical issue in a parish or school may generate hitherto hidden talents for leadership. Our experience tells us that those who organize parish or school liturgies are not necessarily the best leaders in diocesan fund-raising or in organizing parish outreach programs.

A significant shift in leadership theory was observed during the 1980s. Stephen Covey, author of *Seven Habits of Highly Effective People,* describes this shift as a movement from the "personality ethic" to the "character ethic" (p.19). Leadership theory since World War II has been influenced by business and organizational theories. The management model of leadership tended to dominate how we thought about styles and approaches to leadership. Contemporary leadership theories now emphasize that authentic leadership emanates from holistic values and personal integrity. Covey designates this movement as "inside out" leadership, a "character ethic" leadership. These contemporary theories of leadership converge with a vision of Christian leadership based on gospel values. One of the paradoxes in the church today is the not infrequent failure of its leadership to incorporate the gospel heritage and Christian wisdom into its structures and organization, while so-called secular agencies often give more effective witness to a gospel vision of leadership.

Christian Leadership

Christian leadership has its genesis and inspiration in the life and ministry of Jesus. The New Testament writings describe the experiences of early Christian communities in following the way of Jesus. We gain many insights about Christian leadership, which seeks to influence people to promote the reign of God and to enhance the quality of life in all creation, from our study of the gospels and the epistles.

Church leadership is only one dimension of Christian leadership; it is also concerned with transforming society through the power of God's gracious love. The image of head-heart-hand is an appropriate one for Christian leaders, whether their area of authority is the church or civic community. "Head" is the rational, or intellectual, aspect of leadership; "heart" is the expression of compassionate love; "hand" means intentional action for justice. Christian leaders, characteristically, are to be critical: always critiquing structures and practices in society and church in the light of kingdom values, and traditional: augmenting a 2000-year-old tradition of leadership.

Christian leadership exists as more than an abstract theory; it is embodied in the hearts of people on fire with God's love and striving to share God's creative energy with others. The Trinity most aptly describes God, whose very nature is communal and relational. So, too, the Christian leader's authority (derived from the Latin *augere:* to make something greater, to augment, to cause to grow) is communal and relational; it expands the possibilities and work of those subject to it. Thus if the Christian leader uses her position to try to limit the charisms of the Spirit in the community, then the empowering heritage of Christian authority is betrayed. Authority is an enabling influence; it is never an end in itself and certainly not a personal possession. Christ's authority was directed toward healing and teaching about the reign of God.

Shadow Side of Leadership

Even a cursory glance at leaders in society and church through the ages highlights to what degree Christian leadership has fallen short of its ideal. Insight into our own brokenness helps us to cope with the fact of poor leadership. If we acknowledge our strengths and our failures, we can learn to work with leaders who make mistakes. Because leadership in government and church is less than ideal, even dysfunctional, it is helpful to be alert for signs of poor leadership. I would identify the following as signs of it.

- ignoring or expelling dissenters
- becoming isolated from the community
- allowing subgroups to usurp authority's position
- regarding a position of authority as a personal possession for one's own benefit, rather than as something entrusted to one for the good of others
- stereotyping leadership by engendering uniformity
- losing courage in the face of adversity
- ceasing to use imaginative leadership, causing boredom in the community
- becoming unwilling to consider change
- causing distrust when the leader's words and actions conflict
- considering oneself a teacher, but not a learner
- not nurturing one's spirituality by prayer
- identifying one's worth solely with one's role as a leader
- placing oneself beyond accountability to the community
- becoming apologetic and self-effacing because of a low regard for one's position

These signs of dysfunctional leadership testify to the struggle of leaders to cope with their human limitations and with flawed human and organizational situations. People in church, civic, and business groups need to realize that because leaders are human like themselves, they should not become sacrificial lambs to the projected idealistic fantasies of others. However, periodic evaluations of the effectiveness of leaders are certainly the responsibility of the community. After all, leaders are accountable to the people they serve. They cannot claim immunity from constructive feedback by hiding behind a status wall.

Images of Leadership

Our understanding of the nature of leadership may be illuminated by considering a series of images. The ones suggested here are evocative symbols of good leaders. Which of them appeal to you? What other symbols are meaningful to you?

1. Adventurer is prepared to explore new territory and take risks. By sailing unknown waters, the leader draws maps of uncharted seas.

2. Sage is the wise person who knows the traditions and wisdom of the people.

3. Jester learns to live with the tensions and paradoxes of contradictions; recognizes creative energy within chaos.

4. Myth maker helps the community tell its stories and celebrate its rituals.

5. Bronco buster sits tight as the wild horse kicks and bucks in all directions.

6. Conch holder, as in the tradition of South Pacific cultures, has the authority to speak for the community; acts with vested authority.

7. Prophet has a third eye and sees the big picture; acts as the community's moral conscience.

8. Juggler manages to keep tossing up and catching various balls—family, parish, social life, school, leisure, civic community; keeps all the balls in the air.

9. Keeper of the dream is the deeply respected elder of the community who keeps its dreams and myths alive and articulates its vision.

Models of Leadership

Another way of considering leadership is to propose three models of leadership: managerial, divine right, and holistic.

For much of humankind's history of leadership, the divine right model was the dominant one, namely, leadership was from "above." In our time, the power and influence of the business ethic have enthroned the managerial as the model of leadership.

A holistic (the value of something is more than the sum of its parts) model of leadership proclaims leadership as a cooperative model has its foundational vision in the heritage of the New Testament and is enriched by the insights of contemporary leadership theories. Christians need to ensure that the practice of leadership in the parish, school, or other organization is aligned with the holistic model. To summarize:

1. Managerial emphasizes planning and organization; people are viewed as economic resources; leadership is by control and raw efficiency.

2. Divine right authority is derived directly from God; no accountability to the community; leadership is from the top downwards.

3. Holistic integrates spiritual values with the wisdom of effective leadership practices; collegial style that incorporates the contributions of the community members, respecting their rights and core values.

Reflection

1. Recall leaders who have previously or are now influencing you in a positive way. What are features of their leadership style?

2. Have you thought about yourself as a leader? You have leadership qualities; specify five positive qualities of your leadership style. Which is your best quality? Which quality would you most like to develop now?

3. Compose a story, parable, or symbol about leadership.

4. Research and record all the expressions of leadership in your parish, school, or place where you work. Which practices of leadership would you most like to affirm? Which ones would you like to see changed?

5. When have you felt good (bad) about leadership? Describe what was happening to you and others at that time.

6. This chapter has presented many ideas about leadership. Compose your own definition of leadership.

Leadership is

_____

_____

_____

_____

_____

Christian leadership is

_____

_____

_____

_____

_____

Sayings about Leadership

Fail to honor people,
They fail to honor you;
But of the good leader, who talks little,
When his work is done, his aim fulfilled,
They will all say, "We did this ourselves."
Lao Tzu

A good leader is one whose followers have confidence in the leader. A great leader is one whose followers have confidence in themselves. Anonymous

Unhappy the general who comes to the field of battle with a system.

Napoleon

How you feel about yourself
directly affects
how you live life,
how you relate to others.
Dorothy Briggs

2

Qualities of Good Leadership

What are your memories about people who have influenced you as leaders? I remember with great affection a teacher in a sugar cane farming community. He was also our Boy Scout leader who organized camps and scouting functions that were not only enjoyable but opportunities for learning about comradeship, teamwork, and living in the wild. He was fair and kind in his dealings with us, and knew how to involve us in interesting scouting activities. Another leader who touched me was a compassionate woman, Mum Shirl. I recall sharing meals with people at the pastoral center and hearing of her caring work among her sisters and brothers, especially the disadvantaged. Her energy and blazing passion for justice generated courage in those who struggled against racism. More recently, I attended the funeral of a pastor whose generosity to the poor was legendary. To the horror of the rectory housekeeper, he would give away his evening meal, without a second thought, to those who came to the door for food.

Sadly too, I have witnessed examples of poor leadership, such as one pastor's stubborn failure to initiate any pastoral planning in a parish, or a school principal whose door literally and figuratively was closed to staff, and communication was by memos only.

Your own experiences in pastoral ministry will no doubt help you identify features of effective Christian leadership. Based on my research and experiences as a consultant to parishes and schools, I propose the following characteristics of a good Christian leader.

Integrity

A leader has integrity if her actions flow from her habitual belief in the self-worth of every person. Integrity—soundness of moral character, honesty with self and others—implies that there is congruence between the leader's words and deeds. A leader's character is manifested in her actions. What a leader does is what a leader is. A leader who is honest and truthful evokes trust in her subordinates. We may disagree with a leader's point of view, but we respect her opinion if we know that this opinion reflects her personal beliefs and is not merely a calculated political stance.

Developing a climate of trust in a group takes time. Stephen Covey describes the process of building up trust as making regular investments in the "emotional bank account," that is, establishing trustful relations through many acts of honesty and integrity. If trust has been betrayed, it is not easily regained. Many a leader has lost the confidence of the group, let us say, by spreading gossip or disclosing confidential information about others. Trust brings people together; distrust drives them apart. A good leader learns not only to be faithful to promises made to others, but also to promises made to oneself.

Vision

"Vision" is not any easy concept to communicate because it may evoke images of being unreal or "out of this world." It suggests future hopes and possibilities as well as following a value map. Visionary leadership, which anchors its actions in core values that are life-enhancing, may bring people together by sustaining them through sharing and living a dream. The relentless pressures of surviving each day's administrative headaches can sap a leader's energy. The leader's vision can become buried in mounds of paper and in management crises. If the vision is lost, the parish or school begins to function in a reactive mode when decisions are made as knee-jerk reactions to crises rather than as responses based on guiding principles. When the core values of a school or parish are sucked into the maintenance whirlpool—just keeping the organization afloat—its Christian character is obscured and it becomes just another organization.

A leader may articulate a vision for the group but its legitimacy depends on the degree of ownership by the people. The vision, or value map, of a group emerges from a process of communal sharing. The leader's vision is nothing more than idle rhetoric unless there is a group commitment to all it implies. A pastor or principal may possess an exciting dream for the parish or school, but unless the subordinates participate in certain elements of the dream, the vision remains outside their psychic energy and their enthusiasm for it will be minimal.

The starting point of a leader's vision is a "metanoia," a conversion or paradigm shift in consciousness. Paradigm shifts enable us to see things in a radically new way. In the gospels, Jesus invited his followers to live with the paradox of "the first shall be last and the last first." The metanoia of becoming a disciple is to leave behind our fundamental ignorance of God's mercy and to awaken to and celebrate the abundance of God's loving compassion.

A Leader's Metanoia	**1. Empowering Vision**
	2. Articulating Vision
	3. Illuminating Vision
	4. Nurturing Vision
	5. Celebrating Vision
	6. Mundane Vision
	7. Challenging Vision
	8. Transforming Vision

This chart, developed and modified by R.J. Starratt, is a useful framework to consider various aspects of leadership and vision and how the two relate.

1. A vision is *empowering* when it enables people to use their talents to achieve their goals.

2. A vision needs *articulation* by the leader and the group.

3. A vision is a *reference point* for all the group's actions.

4. A vision withers away if it is not *nurtured* by study, prayer, and sharing.

5. The group is to *celebrate* the vision through its rituals and culture.

6. The group's day-to-day activities are a reliable *witness* to what matters most to them concerning their vision.

7. A *new vision* will evolve though new questions and challenges.

8. A vision ought to *transform* the group's culture.

The pivotal point for this model of visionary leadership is the paradigm shift, or "metanoia," of the leader who sees with new understanding how God's dream for creation is being realized through our cooperation with the Holy Spirit. Visionary leadership leads a school, parish, or other organization to form coherent answers to these questions: "Who matters?" and "What matters?" (De Pree, p. 36). This kind of leadership anchors the group's activities in the rock of firm beliefs and not in the sands of expedient leadership.

Competence

A good leader gets things done. The most spellbinding rhetoric from a leader does not excuse the leader from being a competent manager. A bumbling leader ferments confusion in a group when breakdowns in communication occur with regularity, promises are forgotten, and schedules are habitually ignored. Most staff members are mature enough to recognize that no one leader may possess all the desired competencies; however, they rightly expect that those in leadership positions have sufficient skills to empower a group to achieve its purpose and know how the system works.

Proficiency may be acquired through participation in leadership programs and seminars. Mentors impart much wisdom and expertise by suggesting how things may be done. Most leadership work is not performed on the public stage but in patiently sticking at nitty-gritty, mundane tasks. A good leader is characteristically a persistent hard worker who is attentive to detail. Care with little matters goes a long way in leaders (Peters, p. 115).

Empowerment

An empowering style of leadership strengthens and encourages others to use their talents for the good of the parish, school, or other organization. An empowering leader celebrates the gifts of people and is humbly aware that some people can do things better than he can. Insecure leaders are threatened by another's expertise and may seek to control expressions of this expertise. If people are encouraged to use their talents, a culture of discerning risk-taking flourishes. Creativity and lateral thinking will generate exciting and innovative possibilities in the community. "Power," referring to the way we influence people, is not a bad word. In a leader, it is ultimately intended to nurture power and talents in others.

Collaboration

Leaders who work *with* people rather than *over* them entrust the future of the group to the cooperative efforts of its members. Collaborative leadership acknowledges that viewpoints other than the leader's offer alternatives for solutions and improvements. Working with staff conveys a feeling of trust and a willingness in the leader to relinquish her perspectives without feeling devalued or inadequate. If there is a climate of mutual gain in the group, then we value differences because these tell us that we have more to learn about a given situation. Collaboration rejects competition or put-downs as a way of relating. Because leaders are human, they also need affirmation about what they are doing. A sense of appreciation for the leader's efforts, it is hoped, will free her to engage in a partnership style of leading.

Durability

A certain durability is a necessary ingredient for effective leaders. Every so often, a leader has to cope with pressures from family, strained relationships in the group, budget restrictions, poor health, staffing problems, and a general feeling of weariness. Leadership is not necessarily about making people happy. I recall the advice of a friend when I had to make a difficult decision as a leader: "Go ahead, Kevin," he said; "you seem to be on the right track with the group, but don't expect all of them to stand up and applaud your decision!"

Group members can make great demands on leaders, who need affirmation and care like the rest of us. I remember working in a school where a young religious sister had just resigned as principal. She had been subject to a constant stream of criticism from townsfolk and parish alike because she did not conduct the school like the previous principal, a legend in the parish. Sister related how she was confronted by her parish priest, a gruff, big-hearted man who was not prone to lavish praise. Asked why she was leaving, Sister said that after three years, she had never been judged successful in her leadership. The pastor rebuffed her: "That's foolish, Sister. I've been here for ages and you are the best thing that has ever happened to this school." At this, Sister blurted out, "Then why, just once, didn't you tell me that I was doing all right?"

There are no easy formulas for being a hardy leader. A healthy self-esteem is a good start. A leader who feels positive about herself is more likely to have greater resilience after setbacks, being more objective about failure. A thin-skinned leader may tend to perceive down times in the group as a personal reflection on her leadership style. A supporting network of family and friends allows the leader to keep failure in perspective. A cutback in the budget or the resignation of the pastoral council does not portend the end of the school or parish.

Tenacious leaders are also patient people. Aaron and Hur held up the tired arms of Moses during the daylong battle until sunset (Exodus 17:8–13). Who holds up your arms during times of prolonged problems and conflict? A strong prayer life provides the spiritual focus necessary in a leader who is pushed and pulled in all directions. Like Paul, a leader knows that hardships (as well as joys!) are integral to the ministry of leadership. In 2 Corinthians (4:7–10) we read:

> We are in difficulties on all sides, but never cornered; we see no answer to our problems, but never despair; we have been persecuted, but never deserted; knocked down but never killed; always, wherever we may be, we carry with us in our body the death of Jesus, so that the life of Jesus may always be seen in our body.

Sabbath Spaces

Sabbath spaces are the times when interiority is nurtured and we reconnect ourselves to our God, to others, and to planet Earth. Sabbath spaces may be experienced for a few quiet minutes while waiting for an appointment or during a longer period of reflection. The creative spaces of sabbath enable us to uncover our addictions and compulsions. The grace of space is a healing balm to an over-scheduled leader. To enter sabbath time is like pausing on a difficult route to consult our map of life. A Zen story illustrates the power of down time and reflection.

A holy man was walking toward town when he found a beautiful jade stone on the roadside. When he reached the marketplace, he took out the jade stone to admire it. A man rushed up and said to the holy man, "Give me the jade stone!" The holy man immediately gave away the jade stone, saying, "Keep it!" The man went away but instead of hoarding the jade stone, he reflected on what had transpired. Next day, he sought out the holy man and pleaded with him, "Holy man, give me the gift of giving away a jade stone."

Contemplative leaders learn to let go, to surrender the many "jade stones" that absorb their energies and distort their relationships. Leaders who lack sabbath spaces plunge recklessly ahead until they hurtle over the cliffs of compulsive activities. The Australian aboriginal concept of *dadirri* captures the sabbath quality. *Dadirri* is inner deep listening and awareness that teaches a person to wait attentively for the Spirit, like parched land awaiting the rain. Sabbath may be experienced in play and fun, in leisure, gardening, prayer, music making, recreational sports, and quiet time with friends. In sabbath, we restore the balance between the three levels of time: *chronos* or measured time, *kairos* or special moment time, and *mystical time* which takes us into the sense of the infinite, the numinous.

Spirituality

The Christian community, through its sacramental celebrations, its communal prayer, its actions for justice, and network of support, provides a religious environment for nurturing religious leaders. A spirituality for leaders grounds the diverse expressions of leadership in a world-view where religious faith brings God, people, and Earth together. It is like an anchor that steadies the ship despite the buffeting of turbulent seas. *Religare* (Latin, to "bind together"), the basis of the word "religion," suggests the reconciliaton of the various paradoxes of life into a holistic meaning system, unifying all aspects of life "in Christ."

Strategic Planning

Effective leaders plan for the future as well as address current issues. They anticipate what needs to be done and set plans (and people) in motion, rather than let others set the agenda for the parish, school, or other organization. Carl Jung summed up a useful dictum for proactive leaders in his statement: Do you want to go through life walking upright, or dragged through it by a series of events?

A lack of strategic planning results in crisis management in the organization. Staff in the school or hospital or people in the parish become frustrated when policies are made on the run without any regard for long-term consequences. Effective leaders engage in planning and initiate discerned actions rather than allow themselves to be overtaken by events that should have been anticipated. Every parish, school, or hospital, for instance, should set yearly goals and three-year goals and monitor the progress of the implementation of these goals.

Relationships

Observing a good leader in action, we notice the number of times he interacts with people. Even in brief encounters, he is attentive to what people are saying. People feel prized if they are listened to and their ideas respected. Nurturing relationships is a major element in the role of a leader. Encouraging staff or parish members to work cooperatively is to acknowledge that everyone has a gift for the common good of the community. A leader fosters healthy relationships by building a culture of respect. No one is to be taken for granted, especially the quiet achievers and people who are close to us. Bennis and Nanus (p. 66) warn us:

We tend to take for granted those to whom we are closest. Often we get so accustomed to seeing them and hearing from them that we lose our ability to listen to what they are really saying or to appreciate the quality—good or bad—of what they are doing.

Differences regarding community direction should be celebrated as a sign that the community has more to learn about the topic. Wise leaders make a special effort to relate to those who oppose their ideas. Relationships—and the direction of the group—suffer if an "in" and "out" group climate develops.

We cannot legislate healthy relationships. Leaders don't issue decrees obliging staff to like and respect one another. Such relationships happen when group members struggle through the pain of misunderstanding and personality clashes in an endeavor to seek reconciliation and love. Interpersonal skills, especially in communications, decision making, and conflict management, are very valuable assets for leaders. However, techniques in facilitating relationships between themselves and subordinates can never substitute for a leader's sense of self-worth. When a leader experiences difficulties in relationships, then he might well consider his sense of self-esteem. His inner peace projects a calming influence on the community.

A good leader wanders about, observing, listening, and engaging in chit-chat. It's more difficult for people to relate to an abstract role rather than to a flesh-and-blood leader who spends some time with them each day or week in conversation. When leaders become chained to their desks, they erect barriers to relationships because most people dislike storming the fortress of bureaucracy. Remote leaders are rarely loved and often misunderstood. When people begin to second guess the motives of secluded leaders, they usually come up with the wrong conclusions. Pressing administrative demands on a leader are a serious impediment to his presence among staff, but more effective delegation or a consistent availability may free up the leader to be about.

Knowing Limits

An old saying, "I cannot climb that hill today; sometimes I cannot climb the hill at all," reminds us that a leader simply can't always do what she would like to do. Our levels of energy, lack of competence, poor health, family commitments are just some of the limiting factors in determining what we can actually do. Accepting the reality of limits is to accept interdependence. There are many tasks that others can do better than the leader, who has to recognize how much she needs others. People are put off by a leader's air of self-sufficiency. A leader's arrogant assumption of skills and knowledge when these are lacking is a disservice to the work of the group as well as an insult to the talented members.

Humility is the recognition of our *"humus,"* our rootedness in the soil, in Earth. Humble leadership inspires others to do their utmost within the limits of their talents. When a leader acknowledges and befriends her limits, the limits lose their power to imprison her imagination. A leader possessed by fear of failure has already capitulated to the enemy, temerity. But the leader's acknowledgment of limits is not an excuse for opting out of the responsibility to improve her skills and knowledge of Christian leadership.

Humor

A good leader takes his work seriously but himself not so seriously. Humor keeps our work in perspective and pricks the balloon of ego inflation. A hearty laugh can defuse an emotionally explosive situation on the staff. The staff jester will enjoy God's special blessings because she kept the staff reasonably sane! I recall an occasion when I was addressing a very large group of parents about the urgency of a school-funding issue. As my speech reached its climax, I cried out, referring to the famous fable about the boy and the wolf, "I'm not just crying "Wolf! Wolf!" As I paused for dramatic effect, a young child yelled, "Woof! Woof!" The crowded hall dissolved in laughter and I stood helplessly tongue-tied on the stage. Perhaps church groups may take the salvation thing so seriously that even God may be feeling nervous about it all. A favorite scriptural image is from the book of Proverbs (8:30) where the mysterious feminine wisdom figure is described this way: "I was beside the master worker, delighting him day after day, ever at play in his presence, at play everywhere on Earth."

Imagination

An imaginative leader is a lateral thinker who sees around corners and surprises us by presenting us with unexpected options.

Imagination is a wonderful treasure chest within us, holding all kinds of exciting possibilities (Harris, Ch. 1). A creative leader breaks open the crusty shells of dull conformity and disturbs the group by the "Why not?" challenge. A good leader helps us to ask new questions, rather than let us settle back with comfortable, closed answers. Groups who lack creativity tend to canonize their own world-view. Parishes, schools, and other agencies can be boring places if imagination is stifled. Lacking creativity, the institution can be lulled to sleep in the cradle of routine and iron-cast predictability.

Imaginative leadership encourages a climate of honest dissent, which offers the group an alternative lens to consider an issue. Closed systems that drive out dissent are not open to the discovery of the Spirit of truth. Parish and school communities might well examine their responses to the dissenting voices. Through a discerned incorporation of dissenting opinions, an organization may reach a more profound truth. A healthy knowledge of history will warn any institution staff to be cautious about being certain that they alone possess absolute truth.

Asceticism

Asceticism is the discipline of defining life's boundaries and faithfully following a path of life that reflects one's core values. Asceticism avoids a diffusion of energy and carefully focuses on one's chosen path, setting limits on time and options in order to follow it. An ascetical leader carefully monitors the allure of addictions, especially the addiction of over-scheduling. Time is a precious commodity. "When God made time, God made plenty of it," we are reminded, even though we may think that sometimes there are never enough hours in the day. Perhaps there is an abundance of time, but it is also a necessary skill to manage it prudently. By choosing to do certain things and not do others, an ascetical leader restricts agenda setting by others. According to James and Evelyn Whitehead (*Method in Ministry*, p. 146):

A Christian time management, as an asceticism, will always be understood as a response to grace, to the invitation to become less scattered and less self-centered, pulling myself up by my own bootstraps or independently structuring time for my purposes. The delicate balance, as in all forms of religious asceticism, is becoming strong, responsible agents for our own lives and simultaneously remaining attentive respondents to a presence that precedes our insights and disrupts our plans.

The concluding sentence of this quote is critical. The discipline of asceticism is not a selfish withdrawal into one's own circle of care, but an openness to be touched by the other. A leader learns to respond to pain but not become so absorbed in trauma that she can no longer function. When a leader feels she is being pulled in all directions, she must take stock of her priorities in scheduling time. Otherwise she quickly becomes an ineffective leader who has ignored the dictates of prudence. With God's grace, we humbly accept our limitations not only of talents but of time as well. We can only do what we can reasonably do. The rest we leave to God's providence and the community's social responsibility.

Self-Knowledge

Personal insight into the life journey gives a leader the psychological strength to celebrate the seasons and passages of the journey and to be companion to others along the way. Probably we have all witnessed the destructive consequences of a leader who is not in touch with his inner self. Group members pay a heavy price for a leader who projects unresolved hurts and unfulfilled intimacy needs onto others. To choose a path with heart is to discover and live by our inner truth. When Jung was asked about the life journey, he described it as descending a thousand stairs until one embraced Truth. A compassionate appreciation of the richness and complexity of the leader's own life journey will empower him to stand in solidarity with the joy and pain of fellow travelers.

An enlightened leader will be aware of his own need for interiority because over-scheduling shrivels the umbilical cord of connectedness.

A life of insight suggests creative responses to the right questions. Unless we are watchful, our life journey is shaped by responses to the wrong questions that arise from anxiety and fear.

It is helpful to listen to the inner questions, especially those that reflect our anxieties: "What if I become ill?" "Can I find employment?" "What is the future of my children?" "Is my leadership fruitful?" The leader's commitment to personal maturation, we hope, is a celebration of how the God of mystery and surprises is really a companion Stranger (see Luke 24:31).

Summary

A consideration of the qualities of an effective leader helps us to highlight several important areas of leadership. No one leader can expect to possess all these characteristics. But personal mastery of these qualities of a leader is not beyond the grasp of anyone who sets her mind, heart, and spirit to the quest.

Reflection

1. Below are qualities of an effective leader. Although you may consider all the qualities vital for a good leader, select the five that you judge most important.

- competence
- relational skills
- spirituality
- sense of humor
- budgeting
- communications
- knowledge of legal matters
- time management
- conflict resolution skills
- integrity
- negotiation skills
- hardiness

Discuss with your peers the reasons for your five choices.

2. Name three people you judge as very effective leaders. List the qualities of each that make them effective.

3. Describe your plan to improve your effectiveness as a leader. What area of personal leadership development are you working on now? Why have you chosen this particular area?

4. Reflect on Jesus as a leader. What qualities of Jesus as leader do you admire? What aspects of his leadership do not attract you?

Sayings about Leadership

If you have a why, you can live with a what.
                    Victor Frankl

I never look at the masses; just begin, one, one, one.
                    Mother Teresa

If you want one year of prosperity, grow grain.
If you want ten years of prosperity, grow trees.
If you want one hundred years of prosperity, grow people.
                    Chinese saying

In times of change, learners inherit the earth, while the learned find themselves beautifully equipped to deal with a world that no longer exists.
                    Eric Hoffer

Efficiency is doing the thing right;
effectiveness is doing the right thing.
                    Peter Drucker

3

Co-Leadership

The age of the "great man or woman" style of leadership is no longer appropriate for a world increasingly interconnected through communications technology, world government, and religious ecumenism. It is now the age of the global village. A few decades ago, leadership in a parish or school was a relatively simple process. The roles of parish priest and school principal were clearly defined by church regulations and community expectations. Today the work of agencies such as parishes, schools, hospices, and soup kitchens is a complex operation involving big budgets, a wide diversity of pastoral needs, a plurality of ministers, significant levels of lay participation, and various expressions of interaction with the local community and government regulating agencies.

Wise designated leaders, such as the pastor, the principal, and the hospital administrator, realize that they cannot exercise leadership entirely by themselves. Good leadership is not an "I" thing, but a "we." The work of a Christian agency is best served by bringing together the gifts and energies of many people. Stephen Covey describes this kind of collaboration as a 1+ 1 = 3, because the result is greater than the contributions of two parties, because the possibilities expand when people pool their talents.

Meaning of Co-Leadership

Co-leadership, or team leadership, is a style of leading in which one leader seeks to be partner and companion with another or others in achieving the goals of the organization. Although Canon Law specifies the role of the pastor, and Catholic education offices formulate role descriptions of senior management, and pastoral council constitutions define the roles of council members, co-leadership's contribution emphasizes the power of a cooperative approach, a working *with*, rather than *over*, as the way in which leadership functions best. The multi-disciplined and multi-functional nature of social systems such as a parish or school render the concept and practice of a single leader increasingly obsolete. Co-leadership, or collegial-style leadership, is a team effort that recognizes and affirms the power of working together, rather than a domination style of leadership, which is based on a leader-follower mode of operation. The format of co-leadership may be a parish staff, a pastoral council, a college executive committee, or any administrative group that chooses to work as a team.

The movement toward co-leadership received its impetus from the social sciences and from contemporary theology. Post-Vatican II theology of the laity highlighted the responsibilities of every baptized person to participate actively in the mission of the church to evangelize and transform society. Co-leadership is a consequence of taking our baptisms seriously; it is not a unwarranted grab for power or a form of pseudo-democracy.

Although the concept of co-leadership may be viewed with suspicion in some church circles, the declining numbers of priests and religious suggest that some kind of co-leadership will emerge, if not by conviction, then by default! The growing pastoral expectations of people in parishes, schools, health care, and social response groups have ensured that no one designated leader can possibly handle the legal, theological, financial, social, and educational aspects of these agencies. An additional factor in the movement toward co-leadership is the increasing challenge to patriarchal church leadership to incorporate the wisdom and talents of women into mainstream church leadership. The Christian community rightly deplores the limits to creative leadership that have been placed on the church by failing to incorporate women into its official ministerial leadership. A new consciousness about equity is sensitizing the Christian community to question the validity of continuing to insist on the criterion of gender as a determinant for ministerial leadership. Far from being a threat to designated leaders, co-leadership is an affirmation of their office and a witness to the mutuality and self-giving love of the Trinity.

My experience as a consultant with many pastoral groups would suggest that, however noble the concepts and ideals of co-leadership, its practice is difficult, although rewarding. The parish and school landscape is littered with the tombstones of co-leadership groups who commenced with great hopes and perished in the crossfire of unresolved conflicts and frustrated expectations. Apart from the expected normal clash of personalities between people involved in co-leadership, our Western culture reinforces very competitive ways of interaction. Our self-worth seems to depend solely on doing things.

Co-leadership assumes an abundance mentality, that is, that there are plenty of opportunities, rewards, needs, and talents to go around for everyone. Those with a scarcity mentality are envious and suspicious, jealously possessive of their talents, their leadership roles, their management empires. People with an abundance mentality rejoice at the success of others and celebrate their gifts. Co-leadership is built on trust; it replaces control with interdependence. It is a risky undertaking because the collaboration it requires exposes team members to being rejected and hurt.

There are growing indications that there will be a further extension of co-leadership as a norm for church leadership. As this movement develops, it will need sound theological foundations as well as structural changes in the church so that members of the Christian community can have greater access to information and increased participation in decision making. Positions of responsibility in the Christian community are not given as a personal possession or as a reward for services, but are commissions of stewardship to serve the community and be accountable to it.

For co-leadership to work successfully, I have identified certain areas that must be addressed by those in co-leadership positions.

Commitment to Co-Leadership

The most basic element in successful co-leadership is that the people involved in the team really want to be in this style of leadership and accept the consequences of its implementation. At the outset, members of the co-leadership team might well ask if this particular group is an appropriate one for co leadership. If it is, then are the people involved prepared to make an intentional commitment to its ramifications? In reality, most members of a co-leadership group bring different levels of personal priorities to the team. One person may see the team as very important; others may give the team a low rating considering the amount of energy invested. A recipe for disaster is the imposition of a co-leadership structure because the idea is deemed to be "a good thing" or it is set up in emulation of a neighboring parish.

Those who are psychologically unprepared for a role in co-leadership can find the dynamics of working collaboratively a threatening experience. If members of the co-leadership team are so steeped in individualized ways of working, then they will need to undergo a radical change in leadership styles or withdraw from the scene altogether. Their participation is erratic and disconcerting to other team members and to themselves. An alternative course of action, less dramatic, is for the team members to patiently nurture the transition from mono-leadership to co-leadership. Ongoing personal and group formation for co-leadership is essential to preserve its integrity.

Spirituality

Co-leadership has a theological rationale in the Scriptures. A faith foundation for co-leadership provides the spiritual cement for collaborative ministry (Sofield and Juliano, Ch. 4). These scriptural passages provide a sampling of biblical themes about co-leadership: pooling the gifts of the Spirit (1 Corinthians 12); Jesus sending out missionaries in pairs (Mark 6:8); the bond of love between disciples (John 15); the respective talents of Apollos and Paul shared for the sake of the apostolate (1 Corinthians 3:5–8); the description of the "koinonia," or partnership, of the early Christian community (Acts 4:32–35); the relationships of the Trinity (John 13–17).

Co-leadership in Christian institutions is much more than a convenient social arrangement; it is an act of faith in the creative energy of the Spirit. A holistic model of co-leadership will ensure that the bonding of faith is nurtured through shared prayer and a trusting exchange of life experiences. A meeting of hearts assists the members of the co-leadership group to focus on the purpose of the institution. Pastoral team and councils, school executives, and the like need to schedule regular times for communal prayer and spiritual formation. The pressures of business and management issues will quickly displace prayer and the way of discernment unless group members are committed to the spiritual dimension of co-leadership. Co-leadership groups should expect to begin their meetings with readings from scripture, quieting music and reflection, and shared prayer. (See, for example, *Weekly Prayer Services for Parish Meetings*, Twenty-Third Publications, 1995.) Any practice of mumbling through a perfunctory "Our Father" before beginning the business of running an institution is to be discarded and replaced by well prepared prayer sessions.

Clarification of Roles

The intricacies of task organization and role descriptions necessitate initial care in formulating role descriptions and regular evaluations of how the actual work of various members corresponds to their stated roles and to the team as a whole. The group itself needs to consider how well it operates within the wider context of the various subgroups. For example: How would a parish team relate to the pastoral council and to the parish? Does the school executive team associate closely with the work of the faculty and staff?

Each member of a leadership team brings her expectations and personal agendas to that group; each has certain perceptions as to how her role is to be fulfilled. Everyone wants some sense of satisfaction in what she does and that the energy expended is for a worthwhile endeavor. Periodic role clarification checks among the group members are very useful and sometimes necessary. Key statements for this role clarification are:

"I see my role as a member of this team (school executive, pastoral council, agency administration) as . . ." Others on the team comment on this role statement by observing, for example, "I see your role on this team as . . ." The various perceptions of the roles are compared for congruence and dissonance.

Team members are also invited to compare the various understandings of how the roles of the team in the parish, school, or hospital are understood. For example, members of the community are invited to respond to this statement: "I see the role of this leadership team as . . ."

A particular concern of the team is to monitor the relationships between the team itself and the institution it serves. It is imperative that the team never become an elitist sub-group removed from the mainstream of parish or school life. Once, a school administration team had an end-of-year dinner in a different restaurant from the school staff because of the poor relationship between the two groups. This is an example of what can happen when there is a breakdown of relationships between the co-leadership team and the group it is supposed to serve. The danger of "them" versus "us" is ever present for a leadership team. If there is no careful monitoring of role perceptions and task allocations, frustrations develop between members, who begin to perceive that "he should be doing this or that." Meanwhile, the unsuspecting team member may be contentedly sailing along, believing that he is doing fine.

Organizational Structure

Effective organizational structures allow leadership teams to engage in their tasks with efficiency. Role clarifications, mission statements, set meeting times, procedures for decision making, conflict management, clarity in lines of accountability, periodic reviews—these are just some of the elements of helpful organizational structures. Every co-leadership structure should be flexible enough to be modified according to changing circumstances and pastoral needs. Dysfunctional team leadership should seek the help of consultants and learn from the social sciences about communication and group management. Although every team may wish for organizational stability, it must ensure that the constitution or charter of the organization does not assume the aura of a stone-etched divine revelation. Charters or constitutions are useful only insofar as they regularize and facilitate the task of the team.

Celebrating

Enjoyable times together help dissolve barriers and foster friendship. Many a problem has been solved over a glass of beer or a plate of pizza. Celebrating the passages of joys and sorrows implies a willingness to relate to people not only as work associates, but as people whom we respect and regard as companions. Group members don't necessarily like everyone on the team, but participation in the laughter and relaxation of occasional social times may dissolve stereotypes and personal blocks to friendship. Perhaps the best recipe for co-leadership teams who are too uptight with one another is to learn to spend time together. Rituals to mark the births, deaths, marriages, sicknesses, retirements, advents and departures are signs of a recognition of companionship among members.

Shared Vision

If those on a leadership team work from a shared vision, a fundamental agreement on core values, there is a better chance of coherence and focus in their approach to organizational tasks. Jesus sought to unite his followers by leading them to follow his dream of the reign of God. The values of the reign of God demanded a radical conversion to a new paradigm of relationships. The gospels record how difficult is the way of discipleship.

Co-leadership is developed by the articulation and sharing of each person's vision. The cumulative team vision intersects with the diverse world-views of people in the institution. Given the wide range of each person's world-views and theologies of church, the process of coming to a shared vision that is really owned by the group is a fairly daunting enterprise. One of the problems to overcome in reaching a consensus is the passivity of some people and their reluctance to articulate their beliefs. Fear of non-acceptance may lead the less secure members to keep their views to themselves. Another hindrance to articulating a shared vision is the imposition of a particular vision by a dominant individual or group. The lack of ownership of a shared vision will show itself when tough times appear; the facade of unity cracks open in times of crisis. Sadly, we often find out what people are really thinking when there are angry interchanges.

Leadership teams formulate their vision in a mission statement and revisit it periodically to check and confirm its authenticity. The daily grind of tasks can absorb the energies of the co-leadership group and may generate a dominant maintenance model of operation unless the group regularly returns to its original charism for inspiration.

Decision Making

While the dynamics of decision making will be discussed in a later chapter, the subject is mentioned here to emphasize the importance of agreeing upon a style of decision making for effective co-leadership. People who are affected by decisions must have some say in their formulation, otherwise ownership of their implementation will be minimal. The styles and procedures for decision making will reflect the quality and depth of the leadership structure. Helping people to specify goals and participate in attaining them invites them to also share resources and information.

An effective process of decision making brings together the richness of left- and right-brain thinkers, intuitives and sensates, extroverts and introverts, vertical and lateral problem solvers. Research by women illustrates the holistic nature of women's knowing. According to Belenky et al., "connected knowing comes more easily to many women than does separate knowing" (p. 229). Those who facilitate the process of decision making need to be skilled in knowing how to use what has been learned from a diversity of thinking styles. An agreed-upon format for consensus making generates a climate of security and avoids the impression of making decisions on the whim of the moment—"ad hoc." Co-leadership groups are encouraged to follow decision making processes faithfully, provided they are in accord with the principles of discernment.

Formation for Co-Leadership

The practice of co-leadership is becoming more widespread as an accepted style of leadership in Christian agencies and leadership in society. Formation for cooperative leadership, then, assumes a greater significance. Most of us have a hefty streak of individualism and only reluctantly relinquish our way of doing things. Our propensity for controlling and preserving our little kingdoms is very human. Learning to be cooperative leaders is an art that is acquired through seminars, skills training, and supervision. Balancing the competing responsibilities of family, religious community, friends, leisure times, and the demands of team leadership involves a disciplined approach to time management. Sound, mature insights into one's sexuality enable both men and women to relate comfortably with each other, without either withdrawal or sexual manipulation. Communication skills and a healthy self-esteem empower members to be attentive listeners and to be assertive when the occasion warrants it. A theology and spirituality for co-leadership anchor the team in a faith perspective for their collaborative ministry.

Appraisal for Leadership Teams

The following questions will be useful to appraise a co-leadership group and serve as a reference point for those who wish to reflect on the effectiveness of their leadership team. Use this as a checklist for your situation of co-leadership.

1. Is there a high degree of commitment by team members to the concept and practice of team leadership?

2. Are the respective roles of the co-leadership members clearly defined?

3. How effective is the co-leadership group in making decisions?

4. What expectations do people on the team have about one another?

5. Do team members share and articulate a common vision?

6. Is the leadership team faithful to nurturing its prayer and spirituality?

7. Are there equal workloads among team members?

8. Does the team set specific goals and understand them?

9. Are these goals understood in the same way by all team members?

10. Is there an agreed format for meetings and other maintenance tasks?

11. How is the faith dimension of the leadership group understood and practiced?

12. How are conflict situations managed?

13. How effective is communication among team members?

14. How do group members manage relationships with those outside the leadership team, for example, family, friends, co-workers, neighborhood?

15. To what degree do group members feel free to express their values, hopes, anxieties, feelings?

16. Do team members support one another, especially in difficult times?

17. What is the level of trust among the members?

18. Do the team members celebrate together?

19. Are the talents and resources of group members fully used?

20. Do the group members really take an interest in one another?

21. Are time and resources allocated to the professional and personal development of team members?

22. What binds (and divides) team members?

23. Does the team conduct regular and comprehensive evaluations of its effectiveness?

24. What are the levels of interaction with the wider community groups, for example, with the parish, school, hospital, social response agency?

25. If this leadership group were to be dissolved, would the work of the institution be curtailed or augmented?

Summary

The movement toward co-leadership is a sign of the Spirit encouraging Christian communities to use the many gifts within the community. The model of the church as the People of God affirms the responsibilities of our individual baptisms. The social sciences demonstrate the power of cooperative leadership, provided it follows certain dictums. It is painful to let go of our desire to control events and to cling to power for its own sake. The rewards of co-leadership, however, are evident if we move from a competitive, individualistic style of leadership to one based on cooperation and partnership.

Reflection

1. Describe any current situation of team leadership in which you are involved or know about. What is happening? How effective is the team in achieving its tasks?

2. After studying the questions for appraisal, compose a list of ten commandments, forbidding what would inhibit good team leadership: "Thou shalt not . . ."

3. Discover three scripture passages that highlight a spirituality for team leadership.

4. What features of co-leadership do you find most difficult? Easiest?

5. Compose a motto for team leadership.

6. What song best expresses for you the meaning of co-leadership?

Sayings about Leadership

In community, we learn that survival does not belong to the "fittest" (understood as the "toughest"). Survival is about learning to fit into our community and how the community fits us.

Matthew Fox

Successful companies have a consensus from top to bottom on a set of overall goals. The most brilliant management strategy will fail if that consensus is missing.

John Young

The hero, whether god or goddess, man or woman, the figure in a myth or the dreamer of a dream, discovers and assimilates his opposite (his own unsuspected self) either by swallowing it or being swallowed. One by one the resistances are broken. He must put aside his pride, his virtue, beauty, and life, and bow or submit to the absolutely intolerable. Then he finds that he and his opposite are not of differing species, but one flesh.

Joseph Campbell

4

Spirituality for Leadership

Spirituality for leadership might best be described by storytelling. Stories connect us to the community and to our origins. Stories image our realities. Our quest for God or God's search for us is the journey toward the One who is life and love. A Sufi story makes a telling point.

> A disciple asked the master what he had received from his experience of enlightenment.
> "Did you become a saint?" inquired the disciple.
> "No," said the master.
> "Did you discover the eternal truth?" persisted the disciple.
> "No," responded the master.
> "Did you gain new insights into the sacred writings?"
> "No," the master replied.
> "Then, tell me master, what happened to you?" begged the disciple.
> The master answered: "I became awake."

Spirituality is becoming awake to our true being, a way of living by which we come to see and understand things as they really are. When we embark on a spiritual path, we become attuned to discovering God in every facet of our lives, not, however, in the manner of a precocious three year old who asked his mother where God is. She answered, "Why, God is everywhere." Thereupon Jack set about on his search for God in every room of the house. He investigated all likely hiding places, calling out : "Hi, God. Are you in there?" Jack was nonplussed that not even a trace of God was to be found. Perhaps we do a lot of calling out to locate God's whereabouts, but do we wait around long enough for divine responses?

Spirituality for leadership arouses leaders to an awareness of the power of the Spirit in the community. A vital spirituality empowers leaders to draw refreshing waters from the wellsprings of a faith that recognizes God's providence in everyday events. If a leader's world-view is suffused with a sense of God's gracious love, then she can more easily synthesize the disparate happenings of each day. Spirituality challenges us to move beyond our self-absorption, to be embraced by the Other, as we see in this Zen story:

A self-important man went to the master for guidance. After the man had spoken of his deeds for some time, the Zen master began to pour a cup of tea. He kept pouring until the tea cup overflowed. The visitor called out, "Stop pouring. The cup is overflowing!" The master replied, " You are like this cup; you are overflowing with yourself and therefore will never find enlightenment." The Lord cannot enter a room that is stacked to the ceiling with the furniture of our ego.

An evocative image of spirituality is offered in the book of Revelation (3:20–21): "Look, I am standing at the door, knocking. If one of you hears me calling and opens the door, I will come in to share a meal at that person's side."

There are many streams of spirituality in our world. Christian spirituality celebrates Jesus as the revealed One from God. The "Abba" God of Jesus is a declaration of God's yearning for intimacy with us. This bond of love generates life. Jesus spoke of his yearning for people to live this life of the Spirit: "I have come so that they may have life and have it to the full" (John 10:10). To follow a path of spirituality is to revere our calling to be co-creators with God's provident care. Christian spirituality draws its inspiration from the story of Jesus the Christ and his dream of the kingdom. The Christian community continues to promote the dream through teaching, witness, service, and worship.

Leadership Spirituality

Although there are universal themes in Christian spirituality, leaders by their position have special roles to fulfill and their spirituality is shaped by the demands of these roles. Apart from particular leadership roles, leaders may be spouse, friend, son, daughter, peer, mentor, mother, or father. All these roles influence the ways in which leaders pursue the spiritual journey. Let us consider some themes that are relevant to a leader's spirituality.

Leader as Servant

Chapter 13 of John's gospel records how Jesus moved from the status position as head of the table, knelt down, and washed his disciples' feet as a sign of servant leadership. People who wash feet are very vulnerable. Jesus' dramatic gesture the night before he died was a confirmation of his repeated lesson to his disciples that they must renounce a dominant mode of leadership and become servant leaders (for example, Mark 10:41–45). The "kenosis" of Jesus, described in the letter to the Philippians (2:6), entails a process of self-emptying. This "emptying" is not an apologetic avoidance of responsibility or denigrating the gift of oneself, but letting go of our defenses against the power of God's love. The medieval Dominican mystic, Meister Eckhart, wrote about this kenosis spirituality: "Therefore if you wish to receive divine joy and God, first pour out your clinging to things. Everything that is to receive must first be empty" (Fox, p. 54). Meister Eckhart spoke about the spirituality of "subtraction," stripping away the layers and layers of ego inflation, our need for success, fame, possessions, prestige—and saying "yes" to God's dream for us.

Because people turn to leaders for support and direction, leaders, often held in public esteem, are especially susceptible to over-identification with the various roles that the system, the culture, and the community can impose on them. A subtle temptation for them is to allow the status and aura of these roles to become a substitute for the real self. I recall being invited to speak to a parish assembly in a small country town in the Midwest. The large crowd began to become very restless when the president of the pastoral council used every device to drag out the business section of the meeting until people from the floor demanded that I be allowed to address the gathering as the guest speaker. Later some people told me that the president was a very controlling person who felt threatened by anyone else assuming a leadership role at "his" meeting.

Letting go of the desire to control is very difficult because leaders may feel that their value as a leader would be diminished. Yet God's grace is most powerful when it touches the real self, not the pseudo self. An act of faith can seem like calling out in an echo chamber. Clinging to God is like climbing a high mountain, shrouded in swirling mists. Sometimes the sunlight breaks through the clouds; at other times, we doggedly climb on, groping our way up the slippery slope. Two of the Beatitudes, "Blessed are the poor in spirit" and "Blessed are the gentle" express this kenosis of self-giving, not self-immolation.

Gospels

The four gospels, composed for four communities to interpret and communicate the Good News of Jesus to them, are a rich source of inspiration and direction for those who exercise Christian leadership. Jesus lived and preached a transformational style of leadership. Let us reflect on leadership themes in each of the four gospels.

Mark's gospel was intended for the small Christian community in Rome, most scripture scholars would agree. During the late 60s it was reeling under a series of body blows to their faith. Three leaders, James in Jerusalem and Peter and Paul in Rome, had been executed within a period of perhaps five years. After the zealot uprising in Palestine, the mother church in Jerusalem was under seige from the Roman military juggernaut. Emperor Nero had instigated the first major persecution of Christians. Mark's gospel, the first to be written, is an encouraging statement about the eventual triumph of the Risen Lord who overcomes terrible sufferings. The mysterious figure of Isaiah's Suffering Servant (Isaiah 42; 49; 50; 53) is a prototype of the suffering Messiah, Jesus (Mark 8:31–38). True leadership is faithful service for others, even at great personal cost to the leader: "For the Son of man himself came not to be served but to serve, and to give his life as a ransom for many" (Mark 10:45).

Luke (4:1) portrays Jesus as led by the Spirit into the desert where, after trial, he is recognized and confirmed as the anointed one. Like Jesus, the leader finds strength in an awareness of being chosen for a mission. In Luke (4:18), Jesus begins his ministry in the synagogue in Nazareth by reading from Isaiah: "The Spirit of the Lord is on me, for he has anointed me to bring the good news to the afflicted." Discipleship and leadership in Luke (10:29–37; 15:4–32) are characterized by a commitment to justice, especially to the poor. The oppressed are special friends of Jesus, whose mercy is universal. Leaders are healers and reconcilers who witness to God's loving compassion.

Matthew's gospel was written at a time when the Jewish Christians had been expelled from the synagogue and were struggling to discover a new identity as a community. Matthew's church, the community to whom he addressed his gospel, seems to have been a mixed group of predominantly Jewish Christians, struggling to reconcile their Jewish heritage with the "new Israel" of the followers of Jesus. They were a church in transition that looked for leadership which honored the Torah while embarking on a new journey of discipleship as followers of Christ. Matthew's Jesus is the authoritative teacher who is to lead them and bring the Law to fulfillment (5:17). Like the scribe described in 13:52, Matthew's community sought to bring out from their storerooms new things as well as old. Matthew's gospel presents leaders with a model of how the process of change can be managed.

John In the Johannine tradition, leadership is an expression of a relationship of love between master and disciples (15:1–5). According to John, leaders should not stand on the status of their office as the source of authority but on their intimacy with Jesus. The comparisons between Peter, the office leader, and John are intended to highlight the priority of love over office as the ultimate reference point for the quality of leadership. On three occasions (13:23; 20:8; 21:7), it is John, not Peter, who is next to Jesus at the table or who recognizes the Lord. John also proposes a kind of collegial leadership that includes women. The Samaritan woman (4:4),

Martha and Mary (11), Mary, the mother of Jesus (19:25–27), and Mary Magdalene (20:11–18) are significant people in the gospel.

Religious Generativity

There is a buzz of purpose in a good parish, school, or other institution. People who work there seem alive and energized. The power of love transforms a place from an agency of work into a community of care. Generative leaders—those who generate enthusiasm, concern, and dedication in their co-workers—nurture interactions between people and offer them visions and dreams. Sterile leaders, on the other hand, cast a pall over the group, generating not enthusiasm and dedication, but disgruntlement, sniping, and resentment. Religious generativity is nourished by prayer, relaxation, and the joy and pain of loving and being loved.

Our sexuality is a powerful driving force toward the creation not only of physical life, but of the life of the Spirit and the psyche. Our sexuality urges us to create, but are leaders aware of the fruits of their potential as leaders? What is the heritage a leader wishes to bestow on the community? There are instances of imprudent monuments to a leader's generativity such as a school expansion program which places intolerable strains on the staff or unnecessary parish debts that cripple programs for evangelization. A leader who is in touch with his or her sexuality harnesses the generative energy so that its passion is directed toward the purposes of the organization.

Two foes of religious generativity are an introspective selfish love that is incapable of real care for others, and an isolated sterility where a leader avoids becoming involved with people. Spirit-quenching leadership is a wet blanket on group morale.

A leader's religious generativity communicates something of the breathtaking mystery of God's gracious love becoming evident in the community (Nouwen, p. 23). The promise of Jesus at the Last Supper is his gift of generativity: "I have loved you just as the Father has loved me. Remain in my love. If you keep my commandments you will remain in my love, just as I have kept my Father's commandments and remain in his love" (John 15:9–10).

The image of shepherd is a symbol of generativity. In Isaiah (40:11), Ezekiel (34:11–16), Luke (15:4–7), and John (10:6–18), the shepherd is faithful to his sheep and leads them to fresh pastures. A leader cannot be shepherd if fatigue and lack of personal intimacy leaves her spiritually and emotionally exhausted. Leadership does have its lonely times, when even God seems to have deserted us, but the leader's support network of family and friends and co-workers will remind her that she too is respected and loved.

Reflection and Relaxation

The sacred myth of creation recounted in Genesis describes creation as attaining its climax on the seventh day, the day of rest. On this day, God paused to smile on a beautiful, bountiful world and declare that creation was "very good." On Sunday or other times of relaxation, the leader can regroup and re-member the sense of connectedness with every living thing. How easy it is to be weighed down with a budget you can't balance, family troubles, staff alienation, or any number of the worrysome situations that confront leaders. Leaders can become so immersed in the rapidity of change and urgency of immediate tasks that the colors of the covenant rainbow of creation fade into the dull grey of monotonous toil.

The story of the monk and the galloping horse tells us something about a leader's fate. A farmer was standing at the gate of his farm when he saw a horse galloping along the road with a monk clinging for dear life in the saddle. As the horse thundered by, the farmer yelled: "Reverend, where are you going?" The monk cried out: "Don't ask me; ask the horse!" Have you, as a leader, ever felt like the monk?

The parable of the sower and the seed reminds us that the seed grows at the same rate while we are asleep as when we are awake (Mark 4:27). Times of quiet reflection or relaxation allow the seeds of wisdom and discernment to sprout. Mary's response to the wondrous events of the birth of Jesus (Luke 2:19) was to treasure all the events and ponder them in her heart. For a leader, there are few opportunities for long periods of contemplation. The opportunity for quiet reflection is experienced mostly in brief times of prayer, gardening, listening to music, walking, just sitting about, or reading. Religious images of "alone time" such as desert, cold mountain, and wilderness are symbols of places where we are dispossessed of the superfluous and encounter Truth. There is no hiding behind the bushes of compulsive activity. Walter Burghardt describes the contemplation as "a long loving look at what is real."

On Sunday, participation in church services may be a significant time for celebrating one's religious faith within a supporting environment of Christian community. Sunday Eucharist is precious time to bring together the experiences of the week through the communal liturgy of Word, Presence, communion, and assembly.

Compassion

As a concept, compassion may suggest feeling warm fuzzies about helping those in need. In practice, compassion exacts a stern price of self-giving in real situations. I'm ashamed to recount the following story of how our actions can fall short of our words about compassion.

On the last leg of a 30-hour flight, a person boarded the flight I was on. He was going home to die from AIDS. He talked incessantly to me about his times with prostitutes in Africa and I found myself outwardly polite but inwardly judgmental. When we reached our destination, I knew I should help him with his large carry-on bag to the terminal. But I did not. A woman in the seat behind me provided that service to the young man come home to die.

Compassion is "suffering with" (Latin, *cum* [with] and *patior* [I suffer]. The "suffering with" is very different from the concept of pity, which implies a patronizing superiority. Compassion is standing in solidarity with our co-workers, our brothers and sisters. True compassion involves displacement; we have to move from a comfort zone to a point of vulnerability. There are rarely quick fixes for serious situations of trauma. In some circumstances the leader can offer solutions or a referral; in others, respectful listening and touching and the gift of waiting are the most appropriate responses of compassion. A leader may be most compassionate when he confronts a person, challenging him to become more responsible for the consequences of his behavior. Be compassionate just as your Father is compassionate, Jesus urges us (Luke 6:36).

Apart from our prayer to the God of compassion, leaders grow in compassion by learning to be more in touch with their own weakness and fragility.

Compassion is also demonstrated in passionate action for justice. While a leader cannot allow himself to be overwhelmed by the sea of pain that surrounds him, he is conscious of the alienation and trauma within the institution he is responsible for. He leads by example in insisting on a code of justice, encouraging staff members to be active in expanding the circle of justice in their homes, communities, and churches. The healing ministry of Jesus offers a model of pastoral care, which joyfully affirms the dignity of every person. The compassionate leader should be able to say: "My dear friends, let us love one another, since love is from God and everyone who loves is a child of God and knows God" (1 John 4:7).

Wisdom

A Christian leader is often pressed to make responsible decisions on complex matters. Through attentive listening, prayer, and reflection, she seeks to follow God's will by wise and prudent stewardship. She has much in scripture on the subject of wisdom to contemplate, to guide her as a leader. Wisdom literature proposes a way of living according to God's law (Sirach 1:25–28). Wisdom cherishes values that are life-enhancing. A wise leader is a discerning person who discovers the path of holiness and is a witness to it. Matthew's gospel portrays Jesus as the wisdom teacher, an attentive listener who reaches decisions through prayerful discernment (Wisdom 7:22–25; Proverbs 8:22–26; Wisdom 13:1–9). Paul described Christ as "the power of God and the wisdom of God" (1 Corinthians 1:24). The beatitudes are presented as eight wisdom sayings about the righteous life (Matthew 5:3–12).

Ministry of Leadership

Ministry is a public service, performed on behalf of the Christian community for the promotion of the kingdom of God. The ministry of leadership is the activity of being called to influence a group to live more fully the implications of being baptized. A question for a Christian leader: Do you consider your leadership role merely as a promotion in a career path or also as a call to ministry? As a leader, when and how do you experience your work each day as a ministry of service? The prevailing industrial climate, with its emphasis on promotions, conditions of employment, and legal contracts, poses a special challenge to leaders. The industrial and commercial work environment is so persuasive and pervasive that a leader has to be both assertive and Spirit-filled to keep the ministry perspective of leadership in the foreground.

The history of Christianity abundantly illustrates how easily the ideals of leadership as ministry become subverted by the temptation to consider one's position of leader as the possession of personal power. Leadership seeks to empower the community, not to stake a claim to exercise exclusive rights to that power. The impetus for leadership as ministry flows from one's personal relationship with God and the official designation by the church community.

Spirituality for Weekdays

William Diehl in *The Monday Connection* (Ch. 1) writes about "Monday Christians" who carry their Christian principles into the arena of the workplace. Christian spirituality is not an exclusive province of Sunday worship or only concerned with the things that churches do. We encounter God where ordinary events of each day are unfolding. Unemployment, sexism, violence, homelessness, corporate greed, and pollution are just some of the evils in a traumatic world crying for moral leadership. Monday Christian leaders do not consign their life into separate compartments (God for Sundays and things of the world for the other days). Life is not neatly divided into "religious" and "secular" categories. The Eucharist, works for justice, family living, leisure, parish work, education, health care, and industrial management—all merge into expressions of a faith-filled world-view. Moral leadership flows from deeply held values that reflect this integrity.

Summary

The themes of spirituality presented in this chapter are not intended as a comprehensive overview of the constituents of an appropriate spirituality for leadership, but rather an illustration of its character. For a Christian leader, the mystery of the Trinity is the core symbol of God's nature. Trinity suggests that the character of leadership spirituality is relational, dynamic, community oriented, empowering, creative, and above all, loving. If a leader is attentive to the spiritual life, then she is more connected to self, God, others, and to Earth. From this connectedness flows a passion for justice.

Reflection

1. Who has influenced your spirituality? How did this person affect your spirituality?

2. Compose your own definition of spirituality.

Spirituality is: _____

_____

_____

_____

_____

_____

3. Recall the person who best epitomizes contemporary spirituality for you.

4. What are some current movements in spirituality that seem to be authentic "signs of the times"?

5. Which themes in this chapter seem to be especially appropriate for those in leadership roles? Which themes for leadership spirituality would you like to add to those discussed in this chapter?

6. How, when, where do you pray?

7. Tell your favorite story about spirituality.

8. Give examples as to how people might bring Christ's presence into everyday life.

9. What color do you imagine best conveys the meaning of spirituality?

Sayings about Spirituality

Spirituality is a concrete manner, inspired by the Spirit, of living the gospel; it is a definite way of living before the Lord in solidarity with all persons.

Gustavo Gutiérrez

So set yourself to rest in this darkness as long as you can, always crying out after him whom you love. For if you are to experience him or see him at all, as it is possible here, it must always be in this cloud.

The Cloud of Unknowing

In spring, hundreds of flowers;
In autumn a harvest moon;
In summer a refreshing breeze;
In winter snow will accompany you.
If useless things do not hang in your mind,
Any season is a good season for you.

Zen saying

5

Skills for Leadership

What a relief it is when we work with leaders who are skilled in getting the job done with minimum fuss and maximum efficiency! People in a parish or school appreciate meetings that finish on time, when goals are set, and team members work together cooperatively. Have you ever worked with a leader who possessed a wonderful vision for the parish or school but drove everyone insane by bumbling incompetence? Leaders require both vision and management skills to be effective. The culture of an institution, large or small, is nurtured when a holistic vision is complemented by expertise in management.

A basic premise of management is to recognize that adults process information in different ways according to their preferences in relating to their external world. Instruments like the Myers-Briggs Indicator highlight the diversity of ways in which people think about issues. Although we need to avoid putting people into psychological boxes, there is an abundance of evidence to suggest that we really do respond differently to external stimuli. Thus a basic leadership skill is to help people in the group make the most of their preferred style of relating to the world, and to develop awareness about the value of differences in enriching the wisdom of the group.

In this chapter I identify a number of basic skills for effective leadership. These skills do not represent a comprehensive overview of leadership competencies, but rather a selection of useful tools for good management.

Managing Change

Generally, most people prefer to stay in familiar territory. They tend to resist change, which moves them beyond a comfortable, ordered way of life into uncharted waters. I like the statement by an unknown author: "The only people who enjoy change are babies with wet diapers." To facilitate change, a leader should keep these suggestions in mind:

- Develop a positive attitude to change; present it as an opportunity to do something better.
- Accept the fact that change is always with us.
- Involve the people who are affected by the change at every step in the process. Ownership of the direction of change almost ensures its success.
- Recognize fears, insecurities, and hopes.
- Affirm the efforts required to change, regardless of how small these efforts may seem.
- Offer rewards for change. The new outcome has to be perceived as better than the previous situation, otherwise there is no motivation for change.
- Before beginning the process of change, know the background of the group. Such knowledge will probably indicate an entry point for the strategy to be used.
- Be prepared to modify the process as it proceeds. Rarely does any plan for change work out in the way it was envisioned.
- Anchor the change in a core vision where values are shared by the group, or at least by most of the group.
- Develop a network of support for the people experiencing change.
- Communicate with the people the reasons for the change, the process being used, and possible outcomes.
- Provide ongoing formation for group members so that they develop the skills and resources necessary to handle the change.
- Try to anticipate the possible areas of resistance and have a plan to overcome it.
- Be prepared to tough it out, but know when to compromise.

- Set achievable goals and regularly check how the process is going.
- Respect people's feelings and sense of self-worth.
- Retain a lively sense of humor.
- Focus on the goals of the parish, school, or other organization. Do not allow personalities to set the agenda for change.
- Pray for guidance of the Spirit.
- Explore opportunities for synergizing.
- Sow seeds for change by sharing literature and research on the subject.
- Because there are often personal casualties in change, support and guidance should be available for those who want it.

If change is well managed, then staff members should feel confident that they will arrive at new solutions more beneficial for the institution.

Communications

Communications are two-way interchanges of messages, sending and receiving information. Good communications, which may be at the personal level or at the systems level, provide a link between people to enhance relationships. Poor communications erect barriers and arouse resentment. Good interpersonal communication will involve the following:

- Be attentive to the non-verbals of communications, for example, physical environment, eye contact, body posture.
- Identify blocks to communications, for example, status block, emotional responses, hidden agenda, preoccupation, projection.
- Listen in a non-judgmental way.
- Seek clarification if the meaning is not clear; don't guess at what was meant.
- Use "I" statements so that the hearers understand that you are owning the message.
- Be sincere in what you say.
- Recognize that a diversity of personality types (introverts,

extroverts, sensates, intuitives) will send and receive messages in very different ways.

- Listen at the feeling level. The real message is often in the feelings expressed.
- Listening is an active process; seek first to understand before being understood.
- Be assertive, but not aggressive, in expressing feelings and points of view.

Good communications within systems (school, parish, hospital) facilitate healthy relationships and expedite the achievement of an organization's goals. You may find the following questions helpful in evaluating the efficiency of communications in your parish, school, or other institution:

- How effective is the basic communications circuit: staff meetings, parish or school newsletter, public address system, staff notice boards, computer network links with various groups?
- Are the roles of the group members clarified among themselves and for the wider community?
- Have role expectations been examined?
- Have clear boundaries been drawn around the scope of the roles?
- Do staff meetings facilitate an honest exchange of ideas?
- Are leaders accessible, or do staff members have to wait for extended periods before they can talk with their administrators?
- Do the people of the parish or school know how to maximize the use of the communication system?
- Are grievance procedures well established and known to all?
- Are people sufficiently motivated to invest energy in ensuring good communications?
- Is information technology (telephones, computers, beepers, answering machines, laser printers, fax machines) used to help communications?

Mutual Gain (Win Win)

When conflict happens, good leaders avoid exercising power over others for the sake of political or personal gain. They search for a resolution of conflict or at least its management. Differences of opinion are seen not as threats to harmony, but as assets for enrichment. Diverse viewpoints tell the community that the picture is not complete. If the differences can be incorporated into the ultimate decision, then the solution has been enriched by additional insights. A win/lose style of leadership results in losers being alienated from owning the decision. They either surrender gracefully, opt out of the implementation of change, or await the inevitable day of payback.

A mutual gain style of leadership assumes an abundance mentality rather than a scarcity mindset. Mutual gain leaders, seeing the big picture, don't indulge in posturing games but work toward the best possible outcome for the institution. They are attentive listeners to various points of view and foster divergent opinions by drawing out each person's insights. The leader makes the most of shared input by synergizing, that is, extracting elements from an array of often conflicting opinions and regrouping the ideas into a holistic solution.

Group Facilitation

Since many tasks of the leader, by definition, relate to managing groups such as school faculty, pastoral council, management teams, parish assemblies, and parents' associations, the quality of interpersonal relations is always a major concern. Jesus devoted much of his ministry to the formation of his disciples. The gospel recounts his struggles to inculcate his vision and the obduracy of the disciples (for example, Mark 9:33–37; 10:35–40).

Group leaders need helpful strategies to assist them and others to interact creatively and achieve their goals. Those involved in leadership will find the following suggestions helpful in the facilitation of group relationships:

- Encourage a shared belief among group members about the positive value of consensus decision making.
- Ensure that the physical arrangement of the room is con-

ducive to positive group interactions. Avoid a top/bottom, or pyramid, seating.

- Plan an appropriate process for each particular group. The levels of personal maturity and education, the stage of group development, the degree of competence in achieving the task are some of the factors that would affect the process used.
- Attend to the two major purposes of a group, namely, achieving its purpose and facilitating healthy interactions.
- Helps to achieve group tasks are:
    - -clarify the purpose of the group
    - -initiate an appropriate process to achieve the purpose
    - -communicate relevant information to facilitate the process
    - -keep to the task
    - -develop possible options
    - -focus on a solution
    - -plan actions
    - -evaluate outcomes and the process.
- Suggestions for fostering good relationships within a group:
    - -welcome people into the group and introduce members to one another
    - -set a climate of respectful listening
    - -creatively manage conflict
    - -establish a group habit of synergizing
    - -encourage members to participate if they so choose
    - -acknowledge differences and use them to accomplish your overall goal
    - -help people to become bonded in the Spirit
    - -establish eye contact with the person(s) you are speaking or listening to
    - -show care for one another.

There are many variations in the character and purposes of groups such as groups for prayer, social justice, pastoral planning, peer support, pastoral councils, school and hospital administration teams, staff meetings. Good leadership helps people to appreciate the value of working together for a common reward.

Meetings

A specific kind of group interaction is the meeting format. How can a leader facilitate successful meetings? These ideas on the organization and management of meetings will be conducive to an effective meeting:

- Clarify the purpose of the meeting.
- Have a competent chairperson.
- Hold the meeting in comfortable surroundings.
- Communicate the time, place, and duration of the meeting.
- Set an agenda that has been formulated by those concerned with the meeting.
- Arrange seating to maximize participation.
- Set a climate of welcome and attentive listening.
- Pray for guidance.
- Keep accurate minutes of the meeting.
- Respect individual differences.
- Protect the shy or timid.
- Encourage a collaborative decision-making style.
- Paraphrase, summarize, and confirm your perceptions.
- Help the group to monitor its effectiveness.
- Start and finish the meeting on time.
- Allow conflict to surface and deal with it.
- Strike a balance between discussion time and moving the meeting along.
- Employ various strategies to achieve the goals, for example, using subgroups, providing reflective time.
- Summarize key themes and agreed-on actions before the meeting closes.
- Set date, time, and place for the next meeting.
- Specify follow-up action.

Meetings are an essential feature of the life of organizations, but never hold them for their own sake. Creative leadership at meetings ensures participation and assists those who are present to develop responsibility for the outcomes.

Problem Solving

A helpful leadership skill is to stimulate a group to engage in problem solving. The pastoral council, for example, may be confronted by a serious division in the parish, a school board may decide to review their enrollment policy, a hospital may face an industrial court action. How does leadership approach the problems? Here is a seven-step technique for problem-solving:

1. Identify the Issue
• Describe the issue as concretely as possible.
• Specify a desired outcome.

2. Force Field Analysis
• What are the forces that help? that hinder?
• Tease out the main issues, but don't get bogged down.

3. Generate Responses
• Propose possible solutions.
• Engage in lateral thinking, which stimulates innovative ideas.
• Record these ideas for consideration.

4. Prayerful Reflection
• Interior listening to hopes, anxieties, what-ifs.

5. Focus
• One or two of the best ideas chosen for planned action.

6. Design of Strategies
• Agreement on sequence of action, people involved, and resources needed.
• Anticipate hindrances to the plan.

7. Review
• Agree on periodic evaluation of the action plan.

This problem-solving strategy may be adapted to the members' maturity level and their skills in working together. Each of the seven steps suggests significant aspects of working through problems confronting an institution.

Discernment

How do groups who profess a Christian ethos arrive at decisions? Do members make decisions according to the strength of factions and lobbies and a manipulation of power blocs? Or do Christian gatherings come to decisions by a process aligned with their belief in the Lord's presence amongst them: "For where two or three meet in my name I shall be there with them" (Matthew 18:20)?

Discernment is the process of seeking to discover God's will through a prayerful reflection on alternative positions. It involves sifting through choices in a search to know what the Spirit is saying to this gathering of people at this time of their lives. It is not an imposed parachute of the Spirit into the assembled group, nor a sprinkling of the deliberations with a spray of holy water, but a thorough investigation of the situation in the light of faith. Proper discernment necessitates research, inquiry, listening, discussions, as well as a prayerful appeal to God's providential care (McKinney, Ch. 5).

A parliamentary model of working may involve manipulation, control, majorities (and minorities), voting and lobbying for power. The discernment, or shared wisdom, model implies working together, a commitment to bringing together the members' insights, a faith orientation, and patience in the struggle to know God's will.

The flow of a discernment session follows these stages:

- Gathering the relevant information
- Setting the climate of prayerful reflection
- Presenting the options
- Clarifying the issues
- Private and communal prayer for guidance
- Sharing feelings, hopes, anxieties
- Presentation of proposals for action
- Discussion and focus on preferred choices
- Testing choices in the light of the Spirit
- Communal modifications
- Acceptance and ownership of choices made

The actual format varies according to the purpose of the discernment, but the key elements of prayer, research, sifting out possible options, and common ownership of the decision are essential dimensions of an authentic discernment process.

Adult Learning

How do adults learn? A wise leader understands principles of adult learning that will have an effect on the overall mission of the institution. The principles listed here offer a guide to adult learning:

- Adults bring to learning situations their life experiences, which are valuable resources.
- Adults generally wish to be involved in their own learning process.
- Although adults may learn more slowly than children, their retention may be more lasting.
- Most adults tend to resist change and are cautious about accepting new ideas.
- Adults like to learn in comfortable surroundings.
- The learning process must be adapted to the levels of readiness of the participants, their education, and their cultural environment.
- Generally the topics for learning need to be immediately relevant to life questions or issues.
- Adult learning appeals to diverse motivations such as obligation, a sense of responsibility, encouragement of others, usefulness of the topic.
- Peer learning by which people teach one another is generally very effective.
- Because of the complexity of competing interests in the lives of people, adult learning needs to be flexible in its format and process.
- A climate of affirmation and welcome encourage those of low self-esteem who feel that they have nothing to contribute.
- Adults' needs range across a whole spectrum of interest areas such as parenting, spirituality, communications, grieving, media, theology, stress management.
- Adults expect not to be treated as children.

Leaders who are faithful to the principles of adult learning enable the members of the parish or school communities to feel respected when they participate in adult faith and life programs. A disregard of these principles is an invitation to alienate people. It is also helpful for leaders to acknowledge that they too are companions in learning.

Developing Christian Community

Leadership has a vital role in contributing to the growth and life of the parish, school, or hospital *as a Christian community*. Leaders help people in these institutions to develop Christian communities by attending to a number of skills associated with nurturing and building them. There are at least three areas to address: having a "map" of Christian community, knowing the stages of community development, and the behaviors of the group members.

1. Community Map The community "map," or overview, of what a good Christian community looks like helps leaders to affirm the healthy elements and to focus on those that need improvement. An appreciation of these elements will give direction and purpose to leadership. These features characterize authentic Christian community groups:

- A vision is shared and articulated.
- People experience caring relationships.
- There is an occasional celebration of rituals and passages.
- Energy is directed toward the institution's goals.
- There are significant levels of participation.
- The community is open to other communities.
- A culture of mutual gain flourishes.
- There is a vital spirituality in the community.
- People invest energy in building community.
- There is a network of support.
- There are effective communications.
- There is relevant professional and personal development.
- There is adequate expertise in the work of the institution.
- The community enjoys creative leadership.
- Pastoral care of the people is an essential concern of the community.

- The community leaders possess skill in conflict management.
- The community is active in planning for change.
- The leaders promote a culture of truthfulness in the Spirit.
- Decision making is done according to a discernment style.

2. Stages of Community Growth A second skill for a leader in developing community is an awareness of the three "stages" in community growth. The three movements do not follow in a lock-step fashion but certainly reflect the dynamics of change in community relationships. The stages are:

- **Explorations:** Members tread cautiously with each other and tend to smooth over difficulties. Communal conformity is emphasized.
- **Challenges:** Confrontations and power struggles emerge among group members as they begin to assert their authority and protect their vested interests.
- **Bonding/Separations:** There is a movement to come together as a community or a standoff where differences are unresolved.

Leaders recognize that to develop community they must help the group move beyond the polite-face stage and be prepared to surface feelings and divergent opinions. They are also aware that unless group members work through their differences they will remain in a state of chaos or they will revert to the polite-face stage where all are nice to one another on the surface. The real issues are shunted to the safety of the boundaries of the group. M. Scott Peck in *The Different Drum* (Chapter 5) has a perceptive discussion of these movements in community development.

3. Group Behaviors What are common behavior patterns for interactions among members of school boards, pastoral councils, parish groups, school and hospital staffs? It is helpful for group leadership to identify such behaviors in order to be more be more effective as facilitators. These behaviors are common to many groups:

- **Facilitating:** helping members to achieve the purpose of the group.
- **Controlling:** exercising power over others to manage the situation.
- **Blocking:** inhibiting the process and diverting its direction.
- **Manipulating:** using people and group agenda for personal gain.
- **Confronting:** surfacing conflict and dealing with different points of view.
- **Synergizing:** bringing together various viewpoints into a holistic solution.

When leaders can name what is happening in a group, they may be better able to help a group achieve its goals. When they are unaware of the dynamics of group behavior, they are powerless to focus its energy toward the achievement of its goals.

Time Management

How do leaders manage time? How do they set priorities about how time is best used? All leaders have the same amount of time, more or less, but they may not always use time to the best advantage. Different personality types will approach time management according to the values they place on various tasks. Some like to plan well ahead and have things organized long before deadlines. Others have a brilliant flair for instant organization and function best on crisis-time management (their motto seems to be: "To plan a day ahead is to miss all the possibilities of the night before"). Some people think the "careful planner" style of leadership is sterile and lacking in flexibility. On the other hand, the "crisis-time" style can induce a high level of anxiety in people. The suggestions offered here may be useful for your leadership style of time management:

- Learn to delegate.
- Set goals and establish priorities.
- Plan ahead and be proactive, not reactive.
- Be flexible.
- Allow for interruptions.

- Pace yourself.
- Allow time for self.
- Develop an efficient reference system for rapid access to information.
- Learn to be present to people and avoid being preoccupied by the next task.
- Learn to say no.
- Live the three levels of time: chronos, kairos, mystical time.
- Balance time with work, family, self, community.
- Allow for personal space to pray and wonder.
- Accept limits of what can be done and can't be.
- Regularly evaluate time management and reschedule if necessary.

Proper time management allows leaders to be effective in getting things done without undue hassles (Cox, pp. 90-100). Beware if leaders begin to echo the refrain "I haven't got time." Spend time in analyzing how you use your time. And don't forget to waste time every now and then by just doing nothing in particular.

Summary

Leadership skills are not just helpful techniques but express deeply held values about the dignity of people, the recognition of the giftedness of members of the community, and the power of the Spirit working through group endeavors. To be skilled in achieving the purpose of the group while enhancing good relationships among members is a valuable attribute of a leader.

Reflection

1. From your study of the leadership skills described in this chapter, which skill gives you the most concern? Devise a plan to improve your proficiency in this skill.

2. Identify three obstacles, or blocks, to effective group interactions. For each block, suggest how you would overcome this obstacle.

3. Giving feedback to others is a delicate matter. They may be hurt or become aggressive. Specify five principles to guide you in giving feedback to others.

4. As a leader, you know that assertive behavior helps protect your rights and is an act of honesty. Formulate key ideas on being assertive.

5. How would you handle situations where the following statements represent important opinions in the institution?
- "We've always done it this way here."
- "You are new here and don't understand how things work."
- "Your ideas sound good, but they are not very practical in this place."

Sayings about Leadership

Work as if all depends on you.
Pray as if all depends on God.

St. Ignatius Loyola

What the Spirit brings is very different; love, joy, peace, patience, kindness, goodness, trustfulness, gentleness, and self-control.

Galatians 5:22–23

6

Leadership Styles

What is the best style of leadership? Do you have a preferred style of exercising leadership? Which leadership styles are you most comfortable with? Which styles repel you? Despite years of research, no personality trait or particular leadership style has been identified as *the* style that makes for good leadership. Wise leaders know that being a good leader involves much hard work in maximizing one's gifts and trying to limit the impact of one's shortcomings. The distinction between leadership and management that is emphasized in the manuals and articles on leadership is somewhat artificial. Management, they write, is about things; leadership is about people. Rather, effective leadership involves a prudent management of resources, while good management certainly implies the facilitation of healthy and productive interactions between group members. The most precious resource of all is the people in the school, parish, hospice, or other institution.

A number of factors influence leadership style. If leadership is concerned with helping relationships between leaders and followers, then leaders will modify their styles according to the levels of maturity of the group, their own personality traits, the balance between getting the job done and the morale of the group.

One approach to describing leadership styles is to differentiate three distinctive styles: authoritarian, laissez-faire, and democratic. Leaders employ a mixture of styles in response to the immediacy of the task and other factors, mentioned above. A crisis in the school, let us say, may warrant instant and direct action. Leaders don't summon committees when the church is burning down. On the other hand, leaders don't modify the curriculum or build a church without a process of consultation with the school or parish community.

A brief listing of the main features of each style will illustrate its characteristics:

Authoritarian
- Decisions are made without regard for other points of view.
- Focus is on the outcomes, not the people involved.
- Leader is aloof from group members.
- Leader develops immunity from feedback.
- There is resentment and a sense of powerlessness in the group.
- Group members feel no ownership of the outcomes.
- In special circumstances this style may be appropriate when direct and immediate action is required.

Laissez-faire
- Leader opts out of decision making.
- Things just drift along without purpose or direction.
- Power blocs emerge among assumed leaders.
- Group morale deteriorates.
- The output of the group is low.
- This is helpful for groups that need space and time to discover the boundaries of their roles.

Democratic
- Leadership is shared.
- There is acknowledgment of the gifts of the group.
- There is ownership of the process and decisions.
- There is mutual respect for all involved.
- In certain situations of crisis a democratic process may delay urgent action.

No one style described above is proposed as ideal for all occasions of leadership, although the democratic is generally preferred. However, one can well envisage circumstances where the people involved with an institution would appreciate the opportunity to mull over proposals so that the appropriate course of action slowly surfaces. In these circumstances, the laissez-faire style of leadership would be the best approach. No doubt you have often witnessed wise leaders who refrain from bringing things to a head by decisive action until there is further clarity in the situation. In the meantime, the leaders are often criticized for "sitting around and doing nothing"!

A flexi-leadership style incorporates the best elements of all three styles. Flexi-leaders adjust their style to suit the nature of the task. An important element in leadership style is a realistic self-assessment of one's strengths and limits for the particular task. They know their own feelings and competencies and, aware of the dynamics of the situation, are willing to modify their approach if necessary. Above all, a leader should be true to himself.

Carey (pp. 30-32) proposes three styles of leadership: interchange, conforming, and transforming. A brief explanation is offered here with some application to leadership in a Christian setting.

Interchange
- There is no personal involvement.
- Leadership is conducted as a transaction without reference to people's feelings.
- Leadership is considered a detached interchange of products, as wages are exchanged for services.
- The job is done without any reference to the feelings of the people involved.

Conforming
- It calls for a dominant leadership that sets rigid boundaries of what is permitted and what is forbidden.
- Loyal followers are rewarded; disloyal members are punished.
- The motto associated with this style is: "Shape up or ship out."

Transforming
- It calls for a value-driven leadership.

- People are united through a common vision.
- It is characterized by integrity.

An interchange style of leadership would be mechanistic, concentrating on getting the job done without consideration of how people feel about their involvement.

Conforming leadership would make it very clear from the outset that there is one leader and only one ("Things will be done my way around here!"). It is a highly centralized model of administration with all decisions made by the designated leader. Dissenting voices are either driven out, suppressed, or marginalized.

Transforming leadership draws people together around a common vision and invites them to achieve the goals of the organization through cooperative endeavors. The talents of all are focused on the common mission.

Another way of describing styles of leadership:

- **Authoritarian** leadership tells people what to do.
- **Consultative** leadership invites discussion but makes final decisions.
- **Empowering** leadership explores options and empowers group members to participate in the collaborative decision.

The twentieth century witnessed a remarkable shift in our understanding of leadership styles. During the first part of the twentieth century, leadership tended to be autocratic, even dictatorial and patriarchal. In the latter part of the century the growing dominance of business and technology in shaping Western consciousness contributed to identifying leadership with management. In church circles, the long tradition of patriarchal and autocratic styles of leadership is gradually being replaced by more of a consensus kind of leadership. Contemporary leadership emphasizes the power of moral leadership where the leadership style is in accord with core values of the leader and the organization.

Good leaders know that their exercise of leadership is influenced by many factors, such as the levels of maturity of the group and the ways in which leadership was experienced by previous leaders. A pastor who succeeds an authoritarian pastor will have to work diligently with the parish to get them involved in being responsible for the pastoral directions and ministries of the parish. Principals who succeed a very laissez-faire style of leadership may have to bide their time before they move to restore order and coherence in the school. People in an organization need time to adjust to different leadership styles. A leadership change can be threatening to psychological stability.

Understanding the Diversities of World-Views

A salient feature of leadership styles is an appreciation of divergent world-views among people in the community. World-views reflect frames of reference in which people construct their views of reality as they perceive it around them. Leaders in schools where teachers have constructed their world-views around teaching for examination results may have to be patient with these teachers before they reconstruct, or redirect, their world-views toward a more holistic understanding of education. Parish leaders likewise will pursue with prudence a modification of world-views about the role of the laity in the church if the previous administration had little regard for the views of the laity. To embrace the implications of baptism by active parish participation is a slow process, especially when many of the parishioners may not even know the implications of their baptism!

Five world-views, illustrating how various world-views are associated with core values and leadership styles, are presented in the chart (adapted from the work of Colins and Chippendale [p. 88]).

World-View	Key Values	Leadership Styles
Alienated person Perception of world as a hostile place	order and system firm control	autocratic promise of security
Institutional person	efficiency	effective management
Independent person	individual freedom	charismatic encouraging talents
Global person	ecumenism unity in diversity	collaborative visionary
Social change agent	peer support justice	servant transforming

Good leaders recognize the indicators of how people perceive reality and try to adjust their leadership style accordingly. They may frequently encounter people who long for strong authoritarian church leadership because they perceive the church is falling apart and that hostile forces are arrayed against the church. Leaders may work with others who perceive the church as a transforming influence in society which works cooperatively with every other agency for the good of the community. As change agents, leaders will strive to modify world-views of members so that the goals of the organization are fulfilled. A maturation of world-views empowers group members to be active in working toward justice, rather than be hobbled by the chains of narrow, immature concerns. Sadly, the moral authority of the church in society is diminished sometimes when it speaks out on issues in a manner that does not reflect the expanse of God's love.

One of the most formidable challenges for leadership is to work with a wide spectrum of world-views without creating divisive factions. One can only admire the skill of leaders in the parish assembly or school-parent sessions who succeed in reconciling very divergent world-views. The process of synergizing attempts to name common concerns and values among the various points of view and fuse these common elements into an agreed-on position without compromising the integrity of the group members.

Summary

Although we acknowledge that leadership styles are correlated with levels of group consciousness and social environment, a servant style of leadership seems to be the most appropriate one for Christian leaders. Servant leadership reflects the ministry of Jesus. "For the Son of Man came not to be served but to serve. . . ." (Mark 10:45). A crunch question for leadership style in the Christian tradition is whether the exercise of leadership is liberating and inspiring. A liberating style of leadership sets people free to realize God's giftedness to them and the community. Such a style echoes the cry of Jesus at the tomb of Lazarus: "Unbind him, and let him go free" (John 11:44).

Reflection

1. Consider your leadership styles. What are their strengths? What are their limitations? What might you do to affirm the strengths of the ways in which you exercise leadership? How might you modify some of the more obvious limits of your style?

2. Observe a number of community and church leaders. Identify their various styles. Which styles seem to be more effective? Why?

3. Meditate on the gospel passage of Jesus and the woman at Jacob's well (John 4:4–42). Notice the leadership styles of Jesus and the woman in various parts of the story.

4. Recall a recent experience when the leadership style in your parish or school was less than helpful. What happened? What might have been done to improve the situation by a more effective leadership style?

Sayings about Leadership

When the time to perform arrives, the time to prepare is past.

Anonymous

To think is easy. To act is hard. But the hardest thing in the world is to act in accordance with your thinking.

Johann Goethe

The art of leadership: liberating people to do what is required of them in the most effective and humane way possible.

Max De Pree

7

Formation for Christian Leadership

Until recently, there was a widespread belief in Christian circles that when a leader was appointed she or he was given the "grace of state" to be a good leader. While in faith we would affirm the power of the Spirit to support Christian leaders, we should expect that leaders would develop their skills and knowledge about leadership from the insights of the social sciences and their religious traditions. A Christian organization cannot ignore its corporate responsibility to develop leaders who embody its core values and goals. If grace builds on nature, then the "grace of state" depends on how well a parish, school, or diocese uses its available expertise to form leaders who have integrated a Christian vision with effective leadership styles. It is a matter of deep concern that some dioceses and parishes are still appointing leaders to church positions without appropriate training in Christian leadership. Even when formation programs do exist, these courses are inadequate. Management training programs are taught without any reference to a Christian ethos of leadership. There is an implicit assumption that the chaplain or religious education team will attend to the "spiritual dimension," as they express it.

My experience as a consultant and teacher in Christian leadership programs is the basis of the following ideas about the philosophy, principles, and approaches for formation in Christian leadership. These ideas are suitable for any Christian institution, although, of course, the duration, focus, and character of the program will be modified according to the needs of the people, the levels of educational readiness, and the work of the particular agency.

Theology of Leadership Programs

The ministry of leadership is a calling by the Christian community through the Spirit to promote the reign of God. An essential feature of Christian leadership formation is the integration of a Christian spirituality of leadership with the theory and practice of good leadership. Christian leadership implies an ongoing conversion to active discipleship. Programs for Christian leadership are holistic when the training is situated within the context of an appreciation of ministry. The values of the dream of Jesus will permeate every aspect of leadership formation. A ministry perspective on leadership also emphasizes the importance of developing leadership skills and sound theoretical models of leadership.

Principles of the Program

These principles provide a foundation for leadership formation:

- Personal and spiritual development of the leader underpins the acquisition of leadership skills.
- Participants in the program are supported by pastoral networks of companion or cluster groups. Companion groups engage in peer learning.
- Leadership training encourages the participants to discover a world-view impregnated with gospel values. The life and ministry of Jesus are wellsprings for the energy of Christian leadership.
- The insights of the program are communicated through peer learning.
- Instruction is applied to life and work situations.
- Participants bring many life experiences to the program.
- Trainees are guided to identify their leadership styles.
- Formation for Christian leadership encourages participants to bring Christ's presence to every facet of society.
- Holistic learning will embrace not only cognitive information

about leadership, but also affective and imaginative dimen
sions.

Learning Modes

A Christian leadership program, developed according to the principles stated above, may be implemented by using various modes
of learning. Organizers of leadership courses should reject any
model of learning that is simply a series of lectures about leadership. The following modes of learning, tested in many different
kinds of Christian leadership programs, may be modified to ac-
commodate the kind of program envisaged, the people involved,
and their levels of education. Although not all these learning
modes may be used, each mode offers an aspect of holistic learning
that can be incorporated into a variety of leadership programs.

1. Whole Group Contact Sessions In these sessions, the program is introduced, members network with one another in
Christian fellowship, learning units are taught, companion groups
are formed, and reflective writing is experienced.

2. Companion, or Cluster, Groups These are groups of 4-7 participants who meet regularly to share their insights about the program, pray and celebrate together, and teach one another through
peer learning.

3. Learning Module A learning module is a self-study unit of
work by people in their own homes or with a companion learner.
This style of the learning module is adapted to the education levels
of the people and if possible, includes reading, listening to tapes,
and questions for reflection (and discussion if there are more than
one). Learning modules provide opportunities (for example, a series of questions to consider) for personal learning; they emphasize
self-learning.

4. Reflective, or Journal, Writing This mode is a tool to help
people make connections between the events of the day, what is
learned in the leadership course, and one's inner self. If people find
the writing too difficult, they are encouraged to discover other
ways to nurture a sense of interiority. The format of journaling may
be done in words, symbols, or music.

5. Mentors Mentors act as guides and helpful friends to support, challenge, and encourage those in the program to become good Christian leaders. If possible, there is a mentor, or critical friend, for each person in the program.

6. Integrating Presentations These are intended to draw together at regular intervals what has been learned about Christian leadership. The format of integrating presentations may be an oral report, a written assignment, or a group presentation of what was learned. A positive and affirming attitude by program organizers will help to prevent these presentations from becoming threatening to anyone. The standard of these presentations will vary according to the accreditation levels in the diocese, parish, or school.

7. Field Experience A supervised project in leadership training (for example, in parish ministry, health care, social responses, education) grounds leadership theory in the real world where the ministry of leadership is actually experienced. Trainees in the leadership program may work in an edult education team, with a pastoral associate, on a school board, or on a hospital's pastoral care team. At regular intervals, the trainee discusses her progress with the mentor, including what she has learned about Christian leadership.

Coordinating Contact

These various modes of learning allow people to integrate knowledge about leadership with a spirituality that reflects their own life and faith journeys. The length and scope of the program are linked to the needs of a particular institution, the level of accreditation sought, and the resources available. For positions of senior responsibility, the program may extend over one or two years. For school board or pastoral council members, the course may consist of one Saturday and a few evening sessions. Whatever the course length, every organization should insist that there be appropriate formation in Christian leadership for every ministry, including the ministry of priesthood. The program coordinator, who ideally embodies a pastoral and administrative presence, encourages and monitors the effectiveness of the Christian leadership formation.

Content of the Program

What areas of study are useful for Christian leadership programs?

Any number of clamoring voices would insist that one or other topic must be addressed for leaders. I propose six themes for the basic content: leadership, theology, skills for leadership, spirituality, the focused area of ministry (for example, education, health care, parish, disabilities, youth, catechumenate), and field experience. Suggested topics for the various themes are:

Leadership
- definition and description
- styles
- moral leadership
- co-leadership

Theology
- ecclesiology
- revelation.
- scripture
- ministry
- baptism

Leadership Skills
- communications
- groups in action
- conflict management
- facilitating change

Spirituality
- understanding the life journey
- prayer
- everyday spirituality
- action for justice

Ministry
- care of the aged
- school leadership
- school boards
- pastoral council
- ecumenism

- unemployment
- health care
- youth

Field Experience
- parish
- education
- health care
- social responses

An extensive program for Christian leadership provides opportunities for deepening these topics in the participants. Even brief courses may expand the vision of what Christian leadership is seeking to achieve and stimulate trainees to engage in follow-up studies. In parishes of significant multicultural character or low socio-economic environment, the prudence and discretion of program coordinators will adapt these ideas to make leadership formation relevant, practical, and possible.

Technology

Wherever possible, leadership programs should use up-to-date technology to communicate the program's content and to develop supporting networks for the participants. Teleconferences, e-mail, keylink, video conferences are some examples of technological tools that will facilitate learning.

Summary

Formation for Christian leadership—an urgent priority in pastoral planning—is not simply oriented toward serving the needs of the Christian community, but is a transforming presence in a broken world crying out for moral leadership. The emergence of the laity as partners with the clergy in the ministry of leadership is a sign of the Holy Spirit reminding us of the many gifts of the community that have hitherto been generally left idle.

We cannot just assume that people chosen for leadership will automatically be effective leaders. It would be most irresponsible for church leaders, clergy or lay, to fail to implement comprehensive formation of candidates for Christian leadership. Dynamic and imaginative leaders who are passionate about the Good News offer hope and dreams to a jaded world.

Reflection

1. What formation for Christian leadership have you experienced? How useful did you find this formation?

2. Research the programs for leadership development in your institution. What is the program model? Interview some participants in these programs and evaluate how successful the program and courses are.

3. Imagine that you have been invited to prepare a course for Christian leadership. Describe the kind of course you would propose.

4. What has been (is) the most significant thing you have learned about leadership?

Sayings about Leadership

We have met the enemy and he is us.
                              Walt Kelly

On their return the apostles gave him an account of all they had done. Then he took them with him and withdrew toward a town called Bethsaida, where they could be by themselves.
                              Luke 9:10

We must not cease from exploration,
And the end of exploring
will be to arrive where we began
and to know the place for the first time.
                              T.S. Eliot

8

Leadership and Work as Co-Creation

How much work you have done in the last 24 hours, such as getting the children ready for school, preparing budgets, caring for patients, watering the garden, repairing a fence, discussing ways to improve communications in the parish, teaching a class, serving customers in a shop? We spend most of our time working, either in paid or unpaid work. Indeed all creation is busy working. Even the most menial work has value if it is done with skill and commitment. Martin Luther King, Jr., observed:

> If a man is called to be a street sweeper, he should sweep the streets even as Michelangelo painted or Beethoven composed music or Shakespeare wrote poetry. He should sweep streets so well that all the host of heaven will pause to say, "Here lived a great sweeper who did his job well" (Droel and Pierce, p. 46).

The crisis in work in Western society is linked to a number of issues: gender discrimination, unemployment, work that exploits and pollutes the planet, fewer industrial jobs, the growing gap between rich and poor, and numbingly repetitive work. A fundamental question about work is its intrinsic meaning.

- What is the value of human work for us as members of the Earth community?
- Is work merely a means to an end, to purchase things and pay bills, or is our work an expression of a cooperative endeavor to enhance the quality of all life forms in the ecosystem?
- Is work merely a job for material ends, or an act of co-creation with our providential God?

To speak of work as an act of co-creation is not to minimize our wage earnings. We don't live on air! A bank manager would have a bleak view of the inability to pay the house mortgage if the reason was based on "being a co-creator" without an income.

Christian Vision of Work

A Christian leader is intent not only in his support to help people find employment, but in nurturing an appreciation of work as a participation in God's generativity. He seeks to develop an environment for work that is conducive to creativity and just in its economic implications. A religious view of work celebrates it as a manifestation of human beings living in harmony with the dynamic evolution of God's creation. In the words of the twelfth-century mystic Hildegard of Bingen: "When human beings do good work, the cosmic wheel goes around." The word "good" is crucial. Work is "good" if it is friendly to creation, to life in all its forms. An example of "bad" work is the 17 billion dollars spent every week throughout the world on armaments, almost enough financially to provide basic food for all the people on Earth for one year! "Good" work supports the regeneration of Earth's resources, builds community, and provides food and shelter for everyone.

We might ask ourselves if we appreciate our work as an act of co-creation. For example, in my work as a teacher, I hope that my teaching extends the circle of divine wisdom, helps people to develop a sense of noble purpose, and enables students to realize their potential. Whatever work we do—home care, bus driving, banking, farming, nursing—is sacred work if is done with a sense of contributing to the community and to the dignity of humankind. Sadly, some people judge the value of work only in terms of its monetary value or its status on the social ladder. For them, the value of work is set according to its place on the wage scale. A Christian leader might well ponder the mystery of Jesus who spent most of his working life doing ordinary tasks around an obscure village in northern Palestine.

Throughout the ages, Christians have struggled to reconcile conflicting theological attitudes to work. One positive theology of work considers it a contribution to the divine plan for the world. Work, according to others, is to be described as a consequence of the "first sin," described in Genesis. Dualistic heresies, especially Jansenism, taught that the harder the work, the better it was for one's immortal soul. In the sweat of toil, one would concentrate on getting to heaven and leaving behind the valley of tears. In current economic theories, especially capitalism and Marxism, reflecting a mechanistic view of work, humans are reduced to economic cogs in a giant industrial wheel.

In recent decades, Christians are rediscovering a co-creation understanding of work, a development of the Earth community for the benefit of all its members, human and otherwise. Unless we promote a sacred and communal view of work which is accountable to the well-being of the Earth community, we are doomed to experience work only as an economic function. (Little wonder that many workers live for the after-hours time and weekends.) To them, work is only a means to an end, to gain material possessions and social standing.

How might a Christian leader influence people to celebrate work as an act of co-creation? What are relevant themes for a spirituality of work?

Justice in the Ecosystem

This involves more than our behavior and relationships where we work. It also affects the integrity of creation; its goal is to affirm the dignity of people and to preserve Earth's resources for future generations. Because a large proportion of our planet's resources is channeled into supporting the lifestyles of a privileged minority (while millions lack the basics of life to survive), the present rate of consumption is faster than the planet can regenerate them. The cost to planetary health for this is high. Earth is a faithful bookkeeper which is now calling us to account with soil erosion, warming of the atmosphere, salinity, and penetration of the ozone layer. Human technologies are meant to be servants, not masters, of the Earth community.

Justice in the workplace insists that workers and employers exercise basic rights as well as responsibilities—both to each other and to Mother Earth. Ethical leadership will do everything possible to provide employment opportunities and resist corporate "downsizing" of staff in order to maximize inordinate profits.

Work and Recreation

Working people, like Mother Earth, need time and space for regeneration, the opportunity to renew their spirits, enthusiasm, physical strength. The concept of sabbath is not that it is just a day or period of time for rest. It implies an attitude of gently receiving the gift of time as a generative influence toward holistic living. Because we find the long hours and intensity of our work highly stressful, the weekend is intended to provide us with the opportunity for re-creation, a "kairos" time when, with God, we celebrate the wonder and mystery of creation. Vacation time and other time off situate work within the context of ongoing creation. Without such times, we become victims of work and are sucked into the whirlpool of over-scheduling and over-working when anxiety, burnout, and stress-related diseases are its bitter fruits.

Work and Relationships

If we strive to engage in work as a spiritual experience, then we learn to work with others as cooperative partners, not as competitors, and caring relationships in the workplace witness to the love of Christ. A friendly atmosphere at work acknowledges the giftedness of other workers and encourages them to feel that their work is worthwhile. If there is an authentic partnership between women and men at work, then gender discrimination in the workplace is utterly rejected. Healthy working relationships suggest a sensitivity to the various people involved in our work, our families, friends, colleagues, parish, and community. Balancing the competing responsibilities we may have between spouse, family, parent, parish, recreation with the demands of our job requires a regular review of our priorities and how we are fulfilling all our obligations.

Work as a Vocation

Work can be regarded merely as a job for wages or as a vocation. Christian leadership is concerned with enhancing the quality of life in the Earth community. Work is a vocation, the awareness of being called, chosen, to use one's talents to cooperate with God's loving designs for the world. Our job—whatever it is—has value if it contributes to the healing of Earth and its fecundity.

Because technological images, rather than religious ones, have gripped the imagination of Western culture, the distinction between "secular" and "religious" work has become part of our mindset. But this is a false distinction for the person of religious faith (Holland, p. 36). Holistic work does not differentiate between work done for church and work in the factory, office, or home. A spirituality of work is an orientation of our being toward benefitting the Earth community and celebrating the mystery of God's presence. Unless humankind returns to a holistic spirituality of work, then millions of years of Earth's evolution will be discarded within a few centuries of unbridled technology (Berry, Ch. 7).

Ethical leadership supports and contributes to efforts to affect the workplace for a more just society. This kind of leadership encourages people to try to initiate change where they work, no matter how insignificant the change may seem, provided that someone in the Earth community is enabled to live more creatively because of it. Workplace safety practices, sharing jobs, recycling, gender and ethnic equality, harmonious staff relations are examples of how changes in the workplace can enhance the value of work. Good leadership challenges people to be active in their own circle of influence by recognizing work as a vocation.

Imagination

If imagination is the gift allowing us to reconstruct images and symbols, then the energy for holistic work will flow from images that identify us as part of the web of creation. We must dismantle images that see ourselves and our work as *apart from* creation and adopt those that see us as *a part of* it. If our images of work remain locked into a domination model toward Earth, then we will endorse and become part of economic systems that ravage nature.

Christian leaders will join with other discerning voices in the community in the unpopular role of exposing the fallacies of consumerism. We have become so addicted to consumerist images that it will take a sea change for Western industrialized countries to abandon the myth of "steady progress." In the long run, the survival of our planet may depend on our lifestyles being transformed by choosing to live more harmoniously and simply as part of creation.

Summary

By living and fostering a vocational attitude to work, Christian leadership can help followers see their work as an act of cooperation with God's ongoing creation. Everyday work now becomes a sacred endeavor to bring communion and harmony into the Earth community. Although much work is mundane in character and often complex in its relationships, co-creative work is a participation in the challenge of ensuring that the health of the planet and of humankind are inseparable.

Reflection

1. Make a list of all the many tasks you do each day. Which of these do you consider most important? Why? Do you consider some of your tasks more "religious" than others?

2. Explain how your own work might be understood as a co-creative activity.

3. Interview five people about their attitudes toward work. What insights did you gain from these interviews? Did any of the people you interviewed think of their work as a religious activity in some way?

4. Research recent church teachings about work. What are three major themes of contemporary church teaching about work?

5. Specify the kinds of work that are and are not conducive to a healthy planet.

6. Think about the work you do now. How is your spirituality shaped by this work? Do you consider your work as a vocation?

Sayings about Leadership

Without the rich heart, wealth is an ugly beggar.

Ralph Waldo Emerson

We can tell our values by looking at our checkbook stubs.

Gloria Steinem

The richest soil, if uncultivated, produces the rankest weeds.

Plutarch

The heart of leadership has to do with what a person believes, values, dreams about and is committed to, the personal vision. It is a person's interior world which becomes the foundation of her or his reality.

Sergiovanni

9

Leadership for a New Century

Where is Christian leadership heading now? What "signs of the times" are out there that seem to be pointing the way for Christian leaders to interpret? Clearly there are certain themes that recur in books and articles on leadership and in the experiences of effective Christian leaders. Let us explore significant themes and examine their implications for directions in Christian leadership.

Leadership with a New Consciousness

The close of the twentieth century witnessed a paradigm shift of momentous significance for humankind. Many of the features of this leap in consciousness have been described briefly in this book. I designate this emerging era as the "Unitary Age" because of its fundamental character of connectedness. We are becoming more sensitive to the interconnectedness of all creatures in the universe, living and non-living. The destructive powers of dualism that have widened the gap between rich and poor, men and women, first world and third world, black and white, Christian and non-Christian, young and old must be replaced by relationships that emphasize cooperation and interdependence. If leadership can show the way to dismantling the cult of individualism and mechanistic images of our world, helping us instead to re-imagine a world where all live within webs of relationships, then genuine communities will flourish.

A vital role of Christian leadership is to build communities whose loving relationships provide support and pastoral care for the common good of society. Our parishes, schools, and other institutions will flourish as communities if they are not impersonal bureaucracies but genuine gatherings of people who care about one another. Christian leadership must lead the struggle to heal the alienation and fragmentation. The high incidence of family breakdowns is a sign of the difficulties people experience in establishing stable and meaningful relationships. The growing popularity of small Christian communities attests to the longing for more personalized relationships. The values espoused by these communities will almost certainly clash with prevailing cultural values (Whitehead, 1992, p. 122).

A good leader in the Unitary Age will promote a sense of partnership with Earth. The story of humankind will always be incomplete unless its story is viewed as part of the Earth story. The future of humankind is inseparable from the fate of the universe. Fortunately, we are beginning to inch back from the brink of ecological disaster and are racing against time to reverse the consequences of a wanton plundering of the planet's resources. If Earth is a prime manifestation of God's creative powers, then to enhance the integrity of creation is a holy enterprise. Our work is an act of co-creation with the energies of the Spirit. The discerning leader will not mindlessly endorse technology unless it is compatible with planetary health. How can we celebrate the "Word made Flesh" and the "firstborn of creation" unless we reverence Mother Earth? Salvation is not attained on some distant planet but sought in the joys and trauma experienced on our Earth.

Women and Men in Co-Leadership

Co-leadership fosters the spirit of collaboration and the sharing of gifts. Leadership teams in Christian organizations make communal commitments to work in order to achieve their goals. Co-leadership respects the legitimate authority of designated leaders, but it implies a willingness to listen, share, and act cooperatively. People today are less inclined to accept decisions made arbitrarily or by backroom deals. The cultural movement from the experience of authority to the authority of experience is especially challenging for church leadership, which has traditionally operated in a top-down mode (Collins, p. 9). A Christian leader who disregards the implications of this cultural shift will end up talking to herself. If the teaching church is not first a listening church, then it lacks the authenticity of being the voice of the *sensus fidelium*, springing from the lived experience of the faithful.

Christian communities are inclined to take authority more seriously if it reflects the shared wisdom of a discerning people. Co-leadership in a parish empowers people to accept responsibility for what happens there.

Co-leadership, affirming the gospel value of inclusion, invites the Christian community to assume a more radical stance and insist that basic equality stands above privilege in the selection of leaders. Sadly, the church lags behind the wider community's consciousness about women in their societal roles. As long as this situation persists, the official church will have a problem of credibility as a moral leader in its teachings about social justice. We must recognize that patriarchy has distorted the integrity of God's creation. Slowly the church community is coming to realize that systematized patriarchy is a moral disorder. A cooperative rather than a dominating style of leadership challenges the denigrating dualisms noted earlier.

Historical research, the changing economic status of women in society, and a more comprehensive anthropology have exposed the incompatibility of patriarchy with the gospel message. We long for the time when the criterion for Christian leadership will be the giftedness of people rather than their gender.

Leadership in Society

A Christian leader is called to be socially responsible for improving the quality of life in the community, to exert his influence for good causes. We hear of ordinary people who have used political clout to force the legislature to outlaw violent computer games, or of environmental lobbies that have worked to ensure that wetlands were preserved. Amnesty International has saved the lives of thousands of political prisoners. Local business leaders have developed employment programs. Good leadership can make a difference in improving the quality of life for ordinary people.

With many areas of our society in need of healing, a compassionate leader will forge links with coalitions of groups from business, church, media, politics, agriculture, education, and health care to work for the betterment of society. The stretched, thin line of church resources must not try to cover every social need but be a transforming influence to all caring and service agencies in the community. The task of social transformation is a cooperative venture between those who wish to make a commitment toward a more just society. The social teachings of the church provide a rich resource for the directions of moral leadership.

Spirituality for Leadership

There is a yearning to be connected with our psychic roots. The popular fascination with the New Age phenomenon and the relative decline in church affiliations provoke questions about the appeal of the Christian story to the wider community. Is the perceived Christian message really one of Good News? Our cultural longings of the heart are not just a protest against the inability of consumerism to offer anything beyond the cult of hedonism. They express our thirst for wholeness arising out of a religious consciousness. The leadership that speaks to this cultural movement toward spirituality and confronts the hollow tenets of economic rationalism celebrates the sacred story of the covenant between God, us, and Earth. Christian spirituality draws its refreshing waters from the deep well of a 2000-year tradition of those who have sought to follow Jesus in discipleship and experience his presence in the Christian community. Authentic Christian spirituality reverences the diverse ways in which the Spirit has touched the hearts of people in many cultures and religious beliefs.

Everyday spirituality doesn't just happen but is nurtured through prayer, meditation, study, spiritual reading, and intentional action for justice. It does not exist apart from the seasons and passages of life but is woven among the many threads of work and leisure in mundane events. Concretely, the spirituality of a leader is a cohesive force for group members who are buffeted by change, a healing and reconciling presence among them. Only the passionate spirituality of a leader will prevent Christian organizations from being seduced by the mechanistic and consumerist trends of society.

Imaginative Leadership

Philosopher Jürgen Habermas (1984) theorized that there are two basic dimensions of social reality, the "system" and the "life world." The "system" is the objective world of bureaucracies, management, material resources. The "life world" is the symbolic area of cultural values, artistry, and stories of the community. Both "system" and "life world" are necessary for society to function, but a creative balance between the two dimensions must be maintained. Habermas suggests that because of the dominance of commerce in setting norms of a cultural consciousness, the "system" is "colonizing" the "life world." As bureaucracies extend their control and establish iron-clad dictums of political correctness, especially through the power of the media, people feel powerless and alienated. Good leadership seeks to nurture spiritual and human values of the "life world," which give direction to the "system" model of, let us say, the school or parish.

We need courageous artists as leaders who liberate us from images that imprison us into consumerist conformity. With society and church facing grave challenges, who are the imaginative leaders who will help us reconstruct our symbols? One can judge the psychic and spiritual health of an institution by observing what the staff or members do with the prophets and cutting-edge thinkers among them. When school or parish leadership encourages the community to re-imagine and dream, the Kingdom begins to take root and be realized in the community (see Luke 17:21). We cannot fall back on tired solutions that no longer work for the well-being of our society. Dysfunctional leadership strives, or is at least content, to confine our imaginative possibilities and thus betrays the radical reign of God as a symbolic invitation to live differently.

Wisdom Leadership

A wise leader discerns the paths of integrity and reclaims the gospel ideals of leadership (Luke 22:25–27; Mark 10:42–45). The stultifying influence of the technological-industrial model with its emphasis on political correctness is at variance with the teachings of Jesus, the Wisdom teacher. The Beatitudes (Matthew 5:3–12) instruct us that blessedness is earned by choosing a way of compassionate care. Wisdom leadership exposes the limits of electronic illusions and cultural values that denigrate the dignity of humankind and the integrity of creation. Why is the simple life (shopping less and doing with less) considered a threat to the employment rate? To what extent have we become so immersed in consumerism that we have surrendered our gospel vision?

The rapid development of communication technology can overwhelm us with packaged information that interprets experience for us. We can be reduced to the status of passive bystanders who are bombarded with images and messages about happiness, love, security, and wealth. Wisdom leaders learn to evaluate electronic stories from the perspective of Christ.

The eighth Beatitude, "Blessed are those who are persecuted in the cause of uprightness" (Matthew 5:10), reminds us that wisdom leadership must be prepared to pay a heavy price for following a path with heart. Those groups or individuals who are threatened by prophetic challenges tend to punish dissenting voices. If Christian leadership is prepared to follow a way of discernment, then it will discover how the Spirit lives and speaks through the community's faith.

Christian leadership will become more cooperative in style (co-leadership) and be energized by a vibrant spirituality. While its inspiration will emanate from its spiritual tradition, Christian leadership will work, "hands on," with a network of people and agencies to bring healing and hope to the Earth community. Such leadership witnesses to the urgency of Christ's mission: "I have come to bring fire to Earth, and how I wish it were blazing already" (Luke 12:49).

Reflection

1. What evolving trends have you noticed in the styles and practices of Christian leadership? How is your parish, school, or health care agency affected by these trends? What have we gained (and lost) by today's approaches to Christian leadership?

2. Imagine how your organization will be in twenty years. What will be the shape of its leadership structure and style?

3. In what ways is Christian leadership being influenced by changes in society and church?

1. Write your own Credo for Christian Leadership:

I believe: _____

_____

_____

_____

_____

_____

_____

Sayings about Leadership

When we begin to live more seriously inside we begin to live more simply outside.

Ernest Hemingway

If God is for us, who can be against us?

Romans 8:31

In the abundance of his glory may he, through his Spirit, enable you to grow firm in power with regard to your inner self, so that Christ may live in your hearts through faith, and then, planted in love and built on love, with all God's holy people you will have the strength to grasp the breadth and the length, the height and the depth; so that knowing the love of Christ, which is beyond knowledge, you may be filled with the utter fullness of God.

Ephesians 3:16–19

Bibliography

Belenky, Mary F., et al. *Women's Ways of Knowing: The Development of Self.* New York: HarperCollins, 1987.

Bennis, Warren and Burt Nanus. *Leaders: The Strategies for Taking Charge.* New York: Harper & Row, 1985.

Berry, Thomas. *The Dream of the Earth.* San Francisco: Sierra Club Books, 1988.

Carey, M.R. "Transformative Christian Leadership," *Human Development.* Vol. 12, No. 1 (Spring 1991), 30-32.

Colins, C. and P. Chippendale. *New Wisdom: The Nature of Social Reality.* Brisbane, Australia: Acorn Publishers, 1993.

Collins, Pat. *Intimacy and the Hungers of the Heart.* Mystic, Conn.: Twenty-Third Publications, 1991.

Covey, Stephen R. *The Seven Habits of Highly Effective People.* Melbourne, Australia: Business Library Information, 1990.

Cox, Danny with J. Hoover. *Leadership When the Heat's On.* New York: McGraw-Hill, 1992.

De Pree, Max. *Leadership Jazz: Weaving Voice with Touch.* New York: Bantam Doubleday Dell, 1992.

Diehl, William E. *The Monday Connection: A Spirituality of Competence, Affirmation and Support in the Workplace.* New York: HarperCollins, 1991.

Droel, W. and Gregory Pierce. *Confident and Competent: A Challenge for the Lay Church.* Notre Dame, Ind.: Ave Maria Press, 1987.

Fox, Matthew. *Meditations with Meister Eckhart.* Santa Fe, N.M.: Bear & Company, 1983.

Habermas, Jürgen. *The Theory of Communicative Action: Reasons and Rationalization of Society.* Vol. 1. Boston: Beacon Press, 1984.

Harris, Maria. *Teaching and Religious Imagination: An Essay in the Theology of Teaching.* San Francisco: Harper & Row, 1987.

Holland, Joe. *Creative Communion: Toward a Post-Modern Spirituality of Work.* Mahwah, N.J.: Paulist Press, 1989.

McKinney, Mary B. *Sharing Wisdom: A Process for Decision Making.* Allen, Tex.: Tabor Books, 1987.

Nouwen, Henri. *In the Name of Jesus: Reflections on Christian Leadership.* London: Darton, Longman and Todd, 1989.

Peck, M. Scott. *The Different Drum: Community Making & Peace.* New York: Simon & Schuster, 1987.

Peters, Tom. *Thriving on Chaos: Handbook for a Management Revolution.* New York: HarperCollins, 1987.

Sofield, Loughlin and Carroll Juliano. *Collaborative Ministry Skills and Guildelines.* Notre Dame, Ind.: Ave Maria Press, 1987.

Starratt, Robert J. "Human Resource Management: Learning Our Lessons by Learning to Learn" from *Shaping Education.* Carlton Vic. A.C.E., 1986.

Whitehead, James D. and Evelyn E. Whitehead. *Method in Ministry: Theological Reflection and Christian Ministry.* New York: Seabury Press, 1980.

———. *The Promise of Partnership: Leadership and Ministry in an Adult Church.* San Francisco: HarperSanFrancisco, 1991.

Additional Resources on Christian Leadership

In addition to the resources just listed, I wish to express my appreciation for the insights on leadership in these volumes:

Arbuckle, Gerald. *Refounding the Church: Dissent for Leadership.* Homebush, Australia: St. Paul's, 1993.

Avis, Paul. *On Becoming a Leader.* London: Mowbray, 1992.

Bennis, Warren. *On Becoming a Leader.* Reading, Mass.: Addison-Wesley, 1989.

Block, P. *Stewardship.* San Francisco: Berrett-Koehler Publishers, 1993.

Chittister, Joan. *Women, Ministry and the Church.* Mahwah, N.J.: Paulist Press, 1983.

Covey, Stephen R. *Principle-Centered Leadership.* London: Simon and Schuster, 1992.

De Pree, Max. *Leadership Is an Art.* Melbourne: Australian Business Library, 1989.

Dues, Greg and Barbara Walkley. *Called to Parish Ministry: Identity, Challenges, and Spirituality of Lay Ministers.* Mystic, Conn.: Twenty-Third Publications, 1995.

Everett, G.J., et al. *Called to Serve: Reflecting and Visioning about Contemporary Christian Leadership.* Brisbane, Australia: Catholic Education, 1990.

Ferder, Fran and John Heagle. *Partnership: Women & Men in Ministry.* Notre Dame, Ind.: Ave Maria Press, 1989.

Finney, J. *Understanding Leadership.* London: Darton, Longman and Todd, 1989.

Greenleaf, R.K. *Servant Leadership: A Journey into the Nature of Legitimate Power & Greatness.* Mahwah, N.J.: Paulist Press, 1977.

Hickman, Craig R. and M.A. Silva. *Creating Excellence: Managing Corporate Culture, Strategy, and Change in the New Age.* New York: Dutton, 1986.

Kouzes, James M. and Barry Z. Posner. *The Leadership Challenge: How to Get Extraordinary Things Done in Organizations.* San Francisco: Josey-Bass Publishers, 1991.

Marks, Linda. *Living with the Vision: Reclaiming the Power of the Heart.* Knowledge Systems, 1989.

O'Meara, Thomas F. *Theology of Ministry.* Mahwah, N.J.: Paulist Press, 1983.

Senge, Peter. *The Fifth Discipline: Mastering the Five Practices of the Learning Organization.* New York: Doubleday, 1990.

Starratt, Robert J. *Building an Ethical School: A Practical Response to the Moral Crisis in Schools.* London: The Falmer Press, 1994.

_____. *The Drama of Leadership in Action Excursions into Sociology of Action.* Washington D.C.: The Falmer Press, 1993.

Wolski Conn, Joan., ed. *Women's Spirituality: Resources for Christian Development.* Mahwah, N.J.: Paulist Press, 1986.

Of Related Interest...

Called to Parish Ministry
Identity, Challenges, and Spirituality for Lay Ministers
Greg Dues and Barbara Walkley

This book offers lay ministers guidance, encouragement, and support for fulfilling their calling based on the history of the evolving roles of involved lay people in the church. Filled with practical hints on how to minister in the Church, this inspiring book covers such topics as call, enthusiasm, creativity, mission, community, and personal spirituality.

ISBN: 0-89622-649-2, 176 pp, $12.95

The Total Parish Manual
Everything You Need to Empower Your Faith Community
William J. Bausch

In this innovative, imaginative, and empowering work, Fr. Bausch shares ways to make today's parish a vibrant and collaborative community. Covers topics such as sacraments, the liturgical year, volunteers, organizations, small faith communities, evangelization, and more. Here is the complete "how-to" book for guiding a parish to fulfilling its mission. *Awarded first place at the 1996 Catholic Press Association Book Awards.*

ISBN: 0-89622-607-7, 328 pp, $29.95

The Parish of the Next Millennium
William J. Bausch

This renowned author and speaker summarizes the social and cultural forces that shape our lives and our church by pulling together current research and issues that indicate where we are and where we might be going. Divided into three parts, this book catalogues the deep issues dealt with in church and society today, gives concrete signs of hope and rebirth on which to build in the next millennium, and seeks for a posture from which parishes will operate no matter how the structures change.

ISBN: 0-89622-719-7, 304 pp, $14.95